A Life-Changer for Today's Youth

With his national and international success, this author represents a wonderful example of what it means to achieve the American Dream. *Our students at Purdue have benefited greatly from his presentations on campus and from his wisdom and wealth of experience.* If this small-town farm boy from Hoagland, Indiana, could achieve the American Dream, then so can today's youth, regardless of poverty or other difficulties they might have experienced thus far in their lives. Evan Werling is proof that the American Dream is real—but, as stated in this book, it is not free. It must be earned.

MITCHELL E. DANIELS, JR., PRESIDENT
PURDUE UNIVERSITY

This book is an inspirational guide and example of how today's youth, including young women and academic underachievers, can overcome nearly any obstacle in their life and achieve the American Dream.

As an educator, I encourage all of today's youth, their parents, teachers, counselors, and other influencers to read this book, which demonstrates that the American Dream is available to all of today's youth—without exception!

DR. LAURA HAMMACK, PH.D.
SUPERINTENDENT
BROWN COUNTY SCHOOLS

Every young woman and those students who are academic underperformers or who have been bullied should read this book, as they consider their future.

I and many other successful women are proof that all of today's youth can achieve the American Dream—but young women will have a bigger challenge when doing so. The wisdom they will need is discussed in this book. I wish today's youth the very best with their efforts, as they plan their future and their American Dream.

ANGEL

NATIONALLY RECOGNIZED

WOMAN ENTREPRENEUR

This Life-Changing Guide holds the secret for high school students, college students, and entrepreneurs—including young women and academic underachievers, on how they can overcome obstacles in their life and achieve the American Dream.

The author was a small-town farm boy with a poor high school education and no money, who overcame his past, became a CPA and International Entrepreneur, traveled throughout the world, testified before our US Congress, dined with two US Presidents, and received numerous state and national awards. ***His success proves that all of today's youth, without exception, can achieve the American Dream, by following the wisdom contained in this book.***

CRAIG LEE

DECORATED AMERICAN VETERAN

PURDUE ENGINEERING GRADUATE

This book exemplifies the many discussions this author has had with my students. The wisdom and advice in this book are enlightening and have been life-changing and transformative for many young women and for some of those students who were disengaged, were being bullied, or who felt that they had no future. So, have fun and enjoy reading about pursuing your American Dream and the real world that each of us must experience when doing so.

LAURA DAILY
BUSINESS TEACHER
COLUMBUS INDIANA SCHOOLS

This is more than a rags-to-riches story. It tells the truth about the often glossed-over realities faced by entrepreneurs as they struggle to fulfill their dreams. The author's experiences and insights can help everyone prepare for and navigate many of the roadblocks that might be placed in their path as they pursue their own dream. The fact is—*we are all entrepreneurs when it comes to pursuing our American Dream.*

STEVE SAMPSON
ENTREPRENEUR & IT PROFESSIONAL

In every life, when one career door closes, we find that another door opens—if we have the skills, knowledge, and experience to enter through those doors. Make sure your skills and knowledge will lead you to the open doors and to your American Dream—as did the author of this book!

BERNARD J. WEIMER
EDUCATOR AND LEADER OF THE BAND

This book is an excellent example of how a small-town farm boy, with a poor high school education, no money and very little support, achieved the American Dream. It is a powerful guide for helping today's high school and college students understand how they, as the Chief Executive Officer (CEO) of their own life, can achieve the American Dream.

MILLARD AVON GREGORY
AUTHOR OF *SINGLE HARNESS*

I wish my generation had learned these keys to success during our youth. And, I hope that every one of today's young adults will find the truths and wisdom in this book that they need to take charge of their lives and create a future that will lead to their American Dream.

MEMBERS OF THE CLASS OF '57, '63 AND OTHERS

Thank you for sharing the information in this book with me. I paid close attention and chose a business minor to support my education in a technology field. As a sophomore, I was recruited for Internships by several national companies and have another internship already in place for next year.

KYLE JONES

STUDENT

PURDUE AND INDIANA UNIVERSITIES

THE
AMERICAN
DREAM
IS REAL

From a Small-Town Farm Boy, to a
CPA & International Entrepreneur

EVAN A.WERLING

For information about this title or to order other books and/or electronic media, contact the publisher:
TheAmericanDreamIsReal.com
TheAmericanDreamIsReal.usa@gmail.com

ISBN: 978-1-7337814-2-8 (hardcover)
         978-1-7337814-0-4 (softcover)
         978-1-7337814-1-1 (eBook)

Printed in the United States of America

Cover and Interior design: 1106 Design

In Loving Recognition

With love, this book is dedicated to my wife, Angel and the many young men and women who rose from humble beginnings to achieve the "American Dream."

This book is also dedicated to my mother and my wife's parents and grandparents, who loved us and rejoiced in the successes we achieved—and who encouraged us when we hit the rough patches on our journey through life.

Equally important, my wife and I wish to thank the many heroes we met and learned from along the way. As the old adage states: "No man is an island," and few of us can achieve the "American Dream" without help from others. Angel and I learned from many others, as you will read in this book.

Charitable Causes

Net proceeds from this book will be donated to Charitable Foundations and non-profit organizations, such as the Brown County (Indiana) Humane Society and the Purdue University College of Veterinary Medicine.

The Brown County (Indiana) Humane Society maintains one of the highest "Save Rates" in the United States, with 98% of all incoming pets being saved and placed into loving homes, after receiving the medical care and healing they need.

The Purdue University College of Veterinary Medicine is dedicated to excellence in higher education, and is a leader in research to develop cures for cancer and other serious medical problems that afflict both large and small animals.

Both of these organizations represent the highest level of professionalism and excellence in their respective field of animal care and welfare.

I urge each reader of this book to make an effort to help save the lives of abused and abandoned pets. In return, their gratitude will warm your heart.

May God bless the many volunteers who donate thousands of hours each year, to make our communities a more humane place to live—for us and for our pets.

The American Dream Is Real

This book is written to encourage today's youth and those who fail to see a prosperous future, to believe in themselves and think as Entrepreneurs when developing their Career Plan, which I refer to as a Personal Strategic Plan (PSP). *Each of us is an entrepreneur, and we must plan our life accordingly.*

For young adults who are thinking about their future, this book will discuss a number of real-world experiences and challenges associated therewith.

But first, each of us needs to understand that we have control over 80–90% of what happens to us in life. Therefore, it is up to each of us to make sure that we take control and consciously pursue our opportunity to experience *the "American Dream"*—which *must be earned.*

The "American Dream Is Real"—if you are willing to pay the price.

If my life of struggle and achievement is an inspiration for today's young men and women, especially those who are academically in the bottom half of their class or were bullied, then it will have served its purpose, because I was one of those students. Equally important, I hope that young women strengthen their resolve to make sure that they control their future—and not let life's circumstances control them.

If this small-town farm boy from the Heartland of America can rise above his humble beginnings and achieve the "American Dream," then ***you, too, can live the "American Dream"—an experience that is out there, waiting for you.***

Be committed, and have a wonderful time in pursuit of "Your American Dream."

The American Dream is Real

Overview

Part I of this book, "The Heart of the Matter," discusses important realities of life, and defines key fundamentals that everyone will need—if they wish to achieve the "American Dream." Understanding each of these factors is critical, if we are to succeed with our dreams.

Part II focuses on "Important Lessons" that I have learned in life, with the hope that this knowledge will help today's youth make wiser choices and fewer mistakes as they pursue their "American Dream." Those who ignore these important lessons will look back later in life and regret the unnecessary pain they had to endure because they did not pay attention to these realities of life.

Part III is a history of my Entrepreneurial Life, which is proof that the "American Dream Is Real"—*if you are willing to pay the price.* It also provides real-life experiences pertaining to many of the factors and important lessons that are discussed in Part I and Part II of this book.

My life was full of struggle, as I pursued the "American Dream." It was clearly "A Road Less Traveled."

Most importantly, after reading this book, I hope that every young person will clearly understand that no matter how complicated, confusing, or difficult life might have been through high school, everyone can succeed. *No one but you can stop you from achieving the "American Dream."*

Part IV is a passing of the torch to younger generations, with the hope that the information contained in this book will help them achieve their American Dream.

The American Dream Is Real

But, It Is Not Free

You Will Have To Earn It

Contents

PART I
The Heart of the Matter

CHAPTER I

The American Dream

W hat is the "American Dream?"

Many of us envision the "American Dream" as an opportunity to reach for the sky and become highly successful in business, science, education, or in other career or professional endeavors.

It can also be considered an opportunity for each of us to freely develop and apply our God-given talents into a challenging and enjoyable career that will provide our families with a comfortable standard of living, both during our working years and throughout retirement.

Some people believe they are *entitled* to live the "American Dream," just because they were lucky enough to be born in the good ole United States of America, or were born into a family of privilege.

Others believe that, if they can just win a big lottery jackpot, they can live the "American Dream." The fact is that a person's chance of winning a lottery jackpot is so small that it is difficult to understand why anyone would waste their time or money on such a risky and improbable outcome.

My experiences as a CPA and International Business Entrepreneur are that the people who believe they are entitled or hope to hit the lottery jackpot are not being realistic and have little chance of living the "American Dream." Instead, they should be investing in themselves, to prepare for a better career and life.

Interestingly, many successful people don't begin to fully realize that they have lived the "American Dream" until the latter years of their life, when they slow down long enough to look into their rearview mirror and see the many roads they have traveled, the setbacks they have experienced, and the challenges they have overcome during the course of their careers.

For me, achieving the "American Dream" turned out to be many things beyond having an enjoyable and challenging career. My "American Dream" included a never-ending drive to accomplish very difficult professional challenges that my peers avoided, because the consequences for failure (and sometimes for success) were very painful—as I was about to learn.

As you will read in Part III, "My Life as an Entrepreneur; A Road Less Traveled," even succeeding in the face of difficult challenges does not always result in positive experiences. I learned the hard way that life is not always fair, and sometimes our successes are recognized with very unpleasant consequences—when we should have been rewarded for doing an outstanding job!

Experience has also taught me that to truly appreciate the "American Dream," each of us must earn what we achieve. If we do not earn our success, how can we expect to appreciate the price (effort) we had to pay to achieve our goals? Psychologically, each of us knows when we have earned our success, and therefore, we have more respect for ourselves when success happens.

Some people believe that only dishonest people make it to the top. From this book, I hope you will realize that it is possible for honest people to achieve the "American Dream"—without sacrificing their good morals, values, and ethics.

When good people pass from this world, I believe that they do so with a clear conscience and with fewer regrets. So, if you currently have good morals, ethics, and values—keep them. If you don't have good morals, ethics, and values, well—that is a burden you will have to bear, unless you become more enlightened and change your ways. We can lie to others, but we cannot lie to ourselves or to our Creator about our morals, ethics, and values.

With these thoughts in mind, let me take you on a journey into the life of this small-town, Hoagland, Indiana farm boy, who, like his heroes, achieved success without inheriting a dime, without benefiting from grants or scholarships, without lying or cheating his way to the top, without taking credit for what other people accomplished, and without walking over or stabbing other people in the back while traveling on his road toward achieving the "American Dream."

Let Our Journey Begin

CHAPTER 2

Life, In Perspective

L ife is very short. However, when in our youth, it is difficult to comprehend the brevity of our lives—except when we see an elderly relative pass from this life or when we see a younger person die from an incurable disease or tragic accident.

When in our youth, we believe that we will live forever and that we are invincible. Why? Because we have yet to experience the real world that lies ahead.

In the history of our universe, all living humans are about the same age. I know that this comes as a shock to many high school and college students when I speak to them and tell them how much I enjoy being in a classroom with people who are about my same age. But it's true—we are all about the same age.

The Hubble Telescope has allowed scientists to determine that our universe is approximately 13.8 billion years old, while our Earth is approximately 3.5 billion years old.

We humans live for about 80, 90, or 100 years. In relation to the life of our universe or our Earth, humans live a very short life—a life that is equivalent to less than the blink of an eye or the snap of a finger.

This reminds me of a self-penned newspaper obituary that went viral several years ago. In it, Emily Phillips, a longtime public school teacher, said: *"I was born, I blinked, and it was over."* At the end of her life, Mrs. Phillips taught her last lesson—that our lives on this Earth are very short.

So, you see, the main difference between a person in their mid-seventies and a teenager is their level of experience, not their chronological age—because in historic and cosmic perspective, all living human beings are roughly the same age.

In America, we are blessed to have all of the freedom we could want, to develop the talents that have been given to us by our Creator. However, life is not a game; there are no opportunities to replay our life. We get one chance to live our life—from start to finish. So, let's challenge ourselves to achieve our potential. In the end, you will be very glad that you gave this life your best effort.

During my lifetime, I remembered a number of songs that mirror the life that each of us live. One very heart-felt song (on YouTube) is "Turn Around," by Dick and Dee Dee, recorded in 1963. When I hear this song, I play it over and over—as it is a reflection of our lives which pass very quickly, as the mother and father in this song experience. I know that this song might not resonate with all young people, but I can assure you it will tug at your heart by the time you reach the senior years of your life. *Our lives on this Earth pass very quickly!*

Considering the foregoing, I encourage my fellow readers to think more about their future, and give this life their very best effort. Remember, in the annals of time, our lives will be over in less than the blink of an eye.

I would be remiss if I did not provide one additional important fact into this discussion. The foregoing information exists because of Nancy Grace Roman, who died on December 25, 2018, at the age of 93. She was considered to be the "Mother of the Hubble Space Telescope." She earned her doctorate in astronomy from the University of Chicago. During her career, she became the first female executive at NASA, where she also became the chief of astronomy in the Office of Space Science at NASA's headquarters. It was her advocacy that led to the designing and planning for the Hubble Space Telescope. She was the recipient of the NASA Exceptional Scientific Achievement Award and the Women in Aerospace Lifetime Achievement Award. Nancy Grace Roman—you are an American Hero and an incredible role model for today's young women!

Thank You, Astronomers

Edwin Powell Hubble

and

Nancy Grace Roman

CHAPTER 3
Real Life

Many, if not most youth, live in a very sheltered home and school environment, with limited exposure to the real world they will face upon leaving high school or college.

The Statler Brothers memorialized this human dilemma in their song titled "The Class of '57." In this song, the members of the high school "Class of '57" had visions that they *would change the world with their great works and deeds, or that the world would change to meet their needs.* Later, after experiencing the real world, the Statler Brothers reflected on how *"life gets complicated when you get past 18,"* and that life did not turn out the way most of their classmates had dreamed.

And so it was, and still is with many high school classes, because life truly does get complicated when we get past 18 and leave the protection of our parents and high school, or college—to face "Real Life."

Mr. Wonderful on the TV program called *Shark Tank* made several statements about life that are quite humorous, but true. He stated: "Life is tough—and then you die." He also said: "Poo poo happens." I know a lot about poo poo, because my brothers and I shoveled it up every day from our farm animals—which wasn't exactly a fun thing to do. ☺

Yes, life is tough! But, we can influence or control 80–90% of what happens to us in life. Unquestionably, there are some things that we can't control. But, let's focus on the majority of factors that we can control, because we cannot control what we can't control. As Frank Sinatra sang—"That's Life."

Most importantly, *for high school and college students, the decisions they make during the next 5–10 years will determine whether they will have an opportunity to live the "American Dream"* and achieve a secure and comfortable future, or a life that has limited career and financial opportunity. *This observation is especially true for young women*—a topic that I will discuss more thoroughly in the next chapter of this book.

Each student who is a junior or senior in high school or in college should understand that your life right now is very much like a person who aspires to become a major league baseball, basketball, or football player. Those athletes have a very narrow window of time to establish their credentials for success. In most cases, if they have not achieved major-league status within 3–5 years of entering their professional sports environment—their dream career is over!

There are a number of reasons why the next 5–10 years will be critical decision-making times for young adults and students. Those reasons will be discussed further in Part II and Part III of this book, along with other factors that will have a significant impact on what unquestionably will be one of the most important decision-making periods in the life of today's youth.

For High School and College Students

The Next 5–10 Years

Will Be Very Important

CHAPTER 4

Real Life— Young Women

L ife has taught me that *young women have it much tougher than boys*—in many, many ways. Young women need to understand the heavier burden they must carry, so they can be prepared to cope with upcoming challenges.

Not only are women expected to be a good wife and mother, but most are expected to be the family cook, dishwasher, clothes washer, house cleaner, chauffer, grocery shopper, PTA parent, etc. And, if that is not enough, many are expected to work a full-time job, to help pay the bills for their household. So, in the real world, many women actually work two or three full-time jobs!

Much worse, at an early age, many girls find themselves unmarried with children. Others who get married at an early age and have children have a better-than-even chance of getting divorced—while trying to raise their children and while working a full-time job. In many cases, the fathers of the children are nowhere to be found, or they provide little or no support—financial or otherwise. So, for the next 16–18 years, these young women end up raising their children as a single parent, unless they remarry—which also has its challenges.

Now—let's look at this situation from a different perspective. During my entire lifetime, I can't think of a single man who endured a pregnancy or gave birth to a baby. I'll bet you can't think of one either, can you? I hope all young women face this fact—that life can be much tougher for them, unless they are prepared to survive and thrive in the real world. *So girls, make sure you are prepared to take care of yourself and any children you might have.*

This reminds me of the TV show called *The Big Bang Theory,* in which Rajesh Koothrappali's father wants Raj to marry a girl from India, while Raj wants to marry an American girl that he "loves." The father scolded Raj and said that he should marry the girl from India, because *"Love Doesn't Last."*

Well, the truth is that married life doesn't remain the fairytale fantasy that many young people envision, where couples live in wedded bliss, happily ever after.

The fairytale life begins with attraction and romantic love, followed by marriage and the honeymoon stage. I suppose these phases are necessary for the reproduction and perpetuation of our human race. However, following these romantic stages, we settle into real life, where respect for each other, commitment, dedication, and acceptance of adult responsibilities eventually become the foundation for most successful marriages.

Yes, love can last, and it can be wonderful—but it evolves during our lifetime, as we experience the realities of living in this world. It does not remain the wonderland of fairytales and romantic fantasies that we initially experience in our youth. The truth is that *every generation of young adults thinks that they are the first people on this Earth to discover "Love."* And then, they grow up and have to face "Real Life." ☺

As the Statler Brothers said in their song: "life gets complicated when you get past 18." I hope all young adults, especially young women reading this book, will take some time to listen to this song, because it has a very honest message about real life that every young person needs to hear. The world did not change to fit the needs of the "Class of '57." It did not change for my "Class of '63," and you can be certain that it will not change for your graduating class!

Therefore, young women should take control of their lives at an early age. They should get the education or advanced training they will need (beyond high school) to qualify for a job that has the potential to become a well-paying career and provide the financial foundation for their future.

Don't rush into marriage or into making babies—if you want to improve your chances for economic success in life. Instead, look for heroes to inspire your vision of the future. Maybe astronomer Nancy Grace Roman can be one of those heroes that you aspire to emulate. In any event, please don't take the risks that could lead to a difficult life, in which you have limited control over your future and little opportunity to achieve financial stability.

Additionally, please recognize that for married couples, on average, women outlive men of their same age.

When reflecting on our lives, I cannot think of many situations where young men take on tougher challenges than young women—except when it comes to heavy lifting or competing in sporting events, where the male physique excels.

This makes me wonder—were women intentionally created to be the stronger gender, since they have to carry the heavier burden of adulthood throughout their lives?

I think they were. What do you think?

Life Is Not Easy for Young Women

Advanced Training or College is Essential

CHAPTER 5

Victimization

"Life is not fair!"

"I didn't ask to be born!"

How many times have we heard those statements?

Well, I have never met anyone during my lifetime that did "ask to be born." I certainly didn't. Did you?

In today's world, there are dozens of counselors, lawyers, etc. who will comfort their clients by telling them: ***You are a Victim.***

It seems that everyone is a victim in today's society. That's what they told me, because I had been beaten with a belt by my dad (many times), and bullied in school! Well, didn't that make me feel good—to know that I was a "Victim"? Does it make you feel good to know that you are a "Victim"? Maybe so! But, after you and I have accepted the fact that we are a victim—our situation in life hasn't improved one bit, has it? All it does it make us mad at other people. What good does that do for us, or for the world in which we live—Nothing!

So, the question we must ask ourselves is—what is each of us going to do to make our life better? ***The truth is that "Life Is Not***

Fair"—so get over it! No one is going to make your life better. They are too busy making their own life better!

Therefore, it is up to each of us to take control of our future and make those decisions that will improve and build a better life for ourselves and our loved ones. Please, don't play the role of a "Victim," because doing so will never make your life better. *Only by improving our attitudes and taking positive action can we make our life better. No one can do it for us.*

During my professional career, I traveled all over the world—to China, the Middle East, Africa, Europe, Canada, and to Central and South America. I have never visited a country that offers as much opportunity for personal and professional growth as we have in the United States of America. We are living in the greatest land of opportunity that our Creator ever established on this planet.

Having experienced this extensive travel, I fully understand why so many people from other countries want to live here. It is because they realize the incredible opportunities that are available to American citizens. They want to have an opportunity to experience the "American Dream," which is not available to them in their birth country. *These are the world's real "Victims"*—not because of anything they have done, but because of the economic and political environment that exists in many of their countries.

Looking at this another way, how many of our citizens are rushing to leave our wonderful country and flee to other countries of the world? I know of no one—except for a few insufferable, ego-driven actors or actresses who threatened to do so, but never did.

Yet, many Americans who live in this land of opportunity can't see beyond the negativism that is being spewed about by a number of people whose primary agenda is to stir up discord, and focus on "what is wrong with America."

Having said the foregoing, let me explain why America's Free-Enterprise System is so much better than any other economic system in the world.

First, you and I are free to pursue any career we desire. The government doesn't tell us what we can or cannot pursue. This is not true in many other countries.

Second, our Free-Enterprise System forces businesses to constantly innovate, and create better quality, newer technology and better products—all of which results in a better value for you and for me. In fact, in our Free-Enterprise System, if companies don't find better ways to serve you and me—their competitors will, and they will cease to exist. This is why our country provides us with a much higher standard of living than socialism, communism, or any other economic system.

I realize that there isn't a perfect country on our planet, but the United States comes as close to heaven as we will ever experience while living on this Earth. So, don't let negative people control or influence your thinking. It will only result in misery and damage to your future. *Life is short; each of us must focus on positive opportunities—from which we can create a wonderful life for ourselves and for those we love.*

Our Creator truly blessed us by allowing us to be born and/or live in the United States of America. Had our Creator chosen to do so, he/she could have chosen for us to be born in a poverty-stricken country, run by a dictator, where we would have had no opportunity to obtain a good education or pursue a good life.

In Part III of this book, I share some of my international travel experiences. One extended trip into the heartland of China clearly demonstrates the advantage US citizens have over people from many other countries of the world.

Be thankful, and take control of your life. You owe it to yourself to develop your potential. You are the only person who controls your future. You can build a better life for yourself and for those you love—but *only if you choose to do so!*

You and I will never become a "Victim," unless we choose to let ourselves believe that we are a victim—and then use this as an excuse for our lack of progress toward achieving our Personal Strategic Plan.

For high school juniors and seniors, and for college students, please remember—the decisions and commitments you make during the next 5–10 years will set the stage for the remainder of your life. So, plan your future carefully.

Don't become a "Victim." Instead, strive to achieve and live the "American Dream." Remember—*the choice is up to you, and nobody else!*

Life Is Not Always Fair, But

Americans Have Incredible Opportunities.

So—Don't Play the Role of a Victim

CHAPTER 6

Financial Literacy

Surveys indicate that approximately two-thirds of older and middle-aged Americans are living from paycheck to paycheck and are not sufficiently prepared for retirement. More than half of our younger people are already stressed because of their financial situation. These facts should alert every generation about the importance of financial literacy and having the ability to do financial planning.

Unlike seventy years ago, today's high school education merely provides the basic education that we need—to allow us to pursue further technical training at a vocational school or a broader education at a university.

Good careers begin after we achieve advanced education, beyond high school.

Regardless of the training or higher education a person pursues beyond high school, they should be aware that, to advance in many careers, it is important to have a solid understanding of finance, which I call "Financial Literacy."

Financial literacy and financial planning are critical, if we expect to achieve the "American Dream" in our careers and in our personal lives.

During my career, I witnessed many companies and organizations that were in financial trouble because members of senior management did not have a solid understanding of basic financial literacy and how their decisions affected the stability of their organization.

I have also met skilled engineers and other technical people who had reached promotional ceilings in their careers, because they didn't have the education that was needed to handle the financial responsibilities associated with higher-level management positions.

At the same time, I found that people with a good financial background became successful in a variety of management positions, because nearly every activity that takes place in a company or organization has a financial impact on the day-to-day operations of that entity. Financial literacy is the lifeblood that keeps most organizations alive—and keeps families out of financial difficulty.

Because of my financial background, when I took over the leadership of failing companies, I was able to evaluate many problems in manufacturing, procurement, design engineering, sales, and the legal side of businesses. I then took over the direct management of each of the problem areas, while I rebuilt those companies. A good financial education was invaluable in my pursuit of the "American Dream."

Currently, I know a young adult who is pursuing a science degree at Purdue and Indiana Universities He is the only person in his degree program who is also studying for a business minor. By the end of his sophomore year, he was already being recruited for internships—on a national level. The business minor will make a huge difference during the career of this young man! ☺

Therefore, people who pursue advanced training or college degrees in non-business fields would be well advised to study business courses along the way, or for their minor. To do so will greatly enhance their ability to land a great position upon graduation and will benefit them throughout their career.

Financial Literacy Is Not An Option

It Is A Necessity

CHAPTER 7

Your Personal Strategic Plan

*L**ife can happen "To You," or life can happen "For You."*** Although there are some things in life that you cannot control, you can control or influence 80%–90% of the things that will happen to you.

Many of our youth make emotional decisions and life choices based on suggestions or directions from people who are influencers in their life. Later, after they have experienced real life, many are disillusioned with the choices they made, but feel trapped and helpless when trying to redirect their focus.

I was very much like the majority of today's youth, confused and uncertain about my future—with the exception that no one considered me to be "college material." You see, my dad belittled people who had an education beyond high school. He was so anti-education that he wouldn't even let our mother take the continuing-education courses that were required to maintain her license as a Registered Nurse. On our farm, my brothers and I did not get to study until we completed our chores, which included feeding the chickens, pigs, and cows, and after hand-milking a cow for our family's consumption and for sale to neighbors.

For those teens and young adults who are lost when thinking about their future, be comforted with knowing that you are not alone with your fears. Many of us who preceded you had the same feelings of uncertainty and insecurity.

However, as teens and young adults, you need to realize that you have reached that time in your life when the decisions and choices you make during the next 5–10 years will dramatically impact the quality and financial stability of the rest of your life.

I am often asked to explain what it is like to be an entrepreneur. My answer is short and simple. It is no different from everyone else's life—because *each of us is an entrepreneur, entrusted with building our own personal business.*

Each of us is the CEO (Chief Executive Officer) of our life. We all start with the same assets—a body and a brain, given to us by our Creator. The only question is, "What is each of us going to do to optimize our opportunity to live the "American Dream?" *What is your "Personal Strategic Plan?"*

No matter how difficult your life has been thus far, you can live the "American Dream," *if you are willing to pay the price.* I know, because I lived the "American Dream"—despite all of the obstacles and challenges thrown my way.

Now, let's start to develop a "Personal Strategic Plan" for your life.

There are several major factors we should consider when narrowing down our possible career focus, including the following factors:

1. The adult life we would like to live (single, married, children, quality of housing, financial expectations, etc.)

2. The career options we think we might want to pursue, to support our desired life-style

3. The reasons we are considering each of the foregoing options

4. Our special skills/talents that support each career option

5. Limitations that could prevent us from being successful at each option

6. Actions we can take to minimize or eliminate the foregoing limitations

Please don't limit your dreams and plans just because you are being heavily influenced by someone else in your life, or because someone doesn't believe in you. ***It's time to start thinking about yourself and the future you might want!***

There are many sources you can use to research potential careers and broaden your knowledge of the opportunities that are possible in the world-wide economy in which we live.

With today's Internet, you can locate multiple sources that provide high-quality reports regarding education beyond high school. *Two very important factors to consider are the **wages** you can expect and the **demand** in the marketplace for people who have attained the higher education that you wish to pursue.*

These fantastic tools are available to everyone (including parents), to help each of us make better choices concerning our future. These wonderful research tools were not available when I was in high school. But now—you can get them for free, with just the click of a mouse!

Among the best Internet sources are reports from FORBES that document the best and worst paying careers, and the higher education associated with each. Equally important to ***potential*** *earnings* is learning about *demand* for the career options we are considering—both for now and expected in the future. In addition to FORBES, there are other excellent sources that report on pay scales and demand for various jobs in the economy. So, compare several sources when contemplating and developing a specific plan for your future.

The difference in starting pay for various degree programs is staggering! Many training and/or college-degree programs have starting wages that are more than 150% higher than for other types of training or college degrees. For example, someone might receive a starting wage of $30,000 a year, while someone graduating with a degree that is in higher demand might start at a wage of $75,000 per year. From this example, a person starting in the lower-paying career would have to work 2½ jobs to earn the pay of someone starting in the higher-paying job. Unfortunately, these wage differentials do not seem to decrease by the middle of a career. So, *choose wisely!*

The foregoing factors are starting to have an impact on some of the traditional degree programs that are offered at major universities. For example, on March 21, 2018, discussions took place at the University of Wisconsin at Stevens Point, with plans to eliminate 13 majors, including English, philosophy, history, and Spanish. The university wants to start focusing on degree programs such as marketing, management, graphic design, and computer science—all of which have demonstrated "value and demand" and that provide "clear career pathways" for their graduates to achieve success in the real world.

Earlier, I stated that everyone should have a fundamental understanding of basic finance and financial planning. Therefore, your Personal Strategic Plan should include obtaining a solid understanding of financial management and planning. This will provide a significant benefit for those who wish to advance into higher levels of management, leadership, or business ownership. I will expand on this topic later when I discuss my career, which focused on rebuilding failing companies and turning them into industry leaders.

Some careers that seem to be desirable because they are "warm and fuzzy" might lead to a life of financial strain with limited growth opportunity. But, if that is what a person chooses to pursue after doing extensive research into the earnings potential and demand for their chosen education, then they have made a knowledgeable decision based on their personal priorities in life.

Remember, the decisions our youth make during the next 5–10 years will dramatically impact the rest of their lives.

Therefore, today's youth should choose their career path wisely, based on extensive research—if they wish to have control over their future and have the possibility of achieving the "American Dream."

As for me, I can only look back at my poor high school education and wish that I had received the guidance and career counseling that is available to today's youth. Please take advantage of the extensive career research that is easily accessed on today's Internet.

Regarding the foregoing, once you have put the effort into developing a *Personal Strategic Plan—there is a second step that is essential when completing this process. It's called an Action Plan.*

Think about it, our world is filled with people who have good intentions, wonderful dreams, and plans for success, only to grow older and regret their failures and disappointments in life—like the Statler Brothers' "Class of '57," which is a mirror image of thousands of other graduating classes.

One of the main reasons for these disappointments is that many people fail to develop and implement an *Action Plan* that identifies specific, measurable goals that must be pursued, to achieve the dreams contained in their Personal Strategic Plan. In addition to goals, the Action Plan must contain timetables for completing each of the steps that will be necessary for us to achieve our goals.

Developing an Action Plan is absolutely critical, if we are to stay on-track and focused on achieving our dreams—otherwise, our dreams will become lost among the many other issues and concerns that each of us must face on a daily basis.

Successful people have Action Plans and make life happen "For Them." They highly value the 80–90% of their lives that they can control, *and do not let life happen "To Them!"* What will you do with your Personal Strategic Planning?

Choose Your Career Path Wisely

Develop Your Personal Strategic Plan

Complete Your Action Plan

PART II
Important Lessons
for Your Life

CHAPTER 8

It's Not About You—
or Me

This is one of the most important lessons I learned in life. Please remember this section, because it should influence many of your future thoughts and actions.

Psychologist Sigmund Freud spent his life studying the human psyche. A significant portion of that time was devoted to our "Ego." In our youth, and in the lives of adults, many people believe that "Life is all about them." Well, let's put our human life into perspective with the universe in which we live.

On July 22, 2018, the *60 Minutes* TV program held a session with NASA Astrophysicist Amber Straughn, in which she stated that the Hubble Telescope was probably the most transformative scientific instrument ever made by mankind, because it has helped scientists discover that there could be more than two trillion galaxies in our universe—each with at least one hundred billion stars (solar systems), for an estimated total of 200 sextillion solar systems in our universe, of which our sun and planets represent only one such solar system. That places our star in the last zero among the 200,000,000,000,000,000,000,000 solar systems in our universe.

So, not only does our life pass by very quickly in comparison to the life of our universe, but our physical existence in the universe isn't equal to even a single grain of sand on all of our world's oceans and lakes combined.

Further, our knowledge and technical abilities are so limited—that we humans can't even travel to and from other planets within our own solar system, let alone to any of the planets in the other 200 sextillion solar systems in our universe—of which our own Milky Way Galaxy is estimated to have 300 billion such solar systems! This knowledge alone should help everyone put their lives and egos into perspective. Why do we have such big egos? Science has clearly demonstrated that there is more knowledge about the universe and us that we don't know than we can possibly imagine!

Now, I am not saying that humankind is intellectually inferior or stupid. But, it is clear (to me) that, for whatever reason, we have been given a very limited scope of knowledge by the Creator(s) of our universe. Clearly there is a reason for giving us this limited knowledge base. Do you know the reason? I don't!

The foregoing observations and other truths about life have taught me that *one of the most important lessons we can learn during our short life on this Earth is that "It's Not About Me."* That's right, contrary to our desire, the world does not revolve around what you or I want. It revolves around what everybody else wants.

The most important need for all living creatures is to assure their survival. Therefore, each of us must first look out for our own survival before we can help someone else. So, it isn't just ego or selfishness that drives our actions—it begins with our desire for self-preservation and then to gain a higher level of security. This is true with animals and with human beings.

A good example of the need for survival can be found in the airline industry. When giving instructions to passengers concerning how to use an oxygen mask, the flight attendant instructs each adult to put their mask on first and *then* help others who might need assistance. Why? Because if each person doesn't put their mask on first—they might not survive to help others! And so it is with our lives—we must plan for our survival, before we can be of help to others.

Previously, I referenced the Statler Brothers' song "The Class of '57." Many readers who have already experienced life beyond high school will find that this song is a mirror into the lives of their own classmates, regardless of when or from what high school they graduated—because *life is not about what you or I want*—and *"the world will not change to meet our needs."*

The brilliant scientist Albert Einstein once said: *"Only a life lived for others is a life worthwhile."*

So, here is a major secret that I learned about how to succeed:

> *"You can achieve nearly anything you want in life—if you provide others with what they want to improve their lives, and if you do it more efficiently and better than anyone else."*

Therefore, despite what our Ego might tell us, *"It's not about you, or me."* Yet, during my career, I marveled at the many people who thought the world revolved around them, and had their office walls adorned with awards and recognitions they had received. I did none of this. Instead, my recognitions and awards were put away in a closet at my home, until I retired—after which I put them on the walls of my home office, as mementos of my career.

Why did I not display these signs of achievement on my office walls? The answer is simple. First, our future is based on what we do next—not on what we achieved in the past. So, it is not good for us to focus on our past achievements. Second, people didn't care about what I did in the past, and they didn't care to see my "bragging wall." They just wanted to know what I was going to do to make their lives better tomorrow. So, a bit of advice to those who wish to achieve the most with their career—don't display your ego on your office walls. However, professional licenses should be displayed.

Further, during my career, I never once "applied" for awards or recognition. You see, any recognitions or awards worth receiving are those that are initiated by the people we serve, and from those who benefit from our presence in their lives. Peer recognition is how I received the various awards and recognitions that are listed in Part III of this book.

Otherwise, I always searched for ways to reward others who were worthy of recognition.

It's amazing how much we gain when we reach out and recognize other people. This approach can (and will) result in building stronger professional bonds in whatever business ventures or endeavors we pursue. An added benefit was that I never once got criticized for praising or promoting the accomplishments of other people who supported and advised me.

Life Is Not About You—or Me

It's About Helping Others

CHAPTER 9

Nobody Owes You or Me a Living

How did we reach this point in our society when able-bodied people who are not working, think the world (or at least our government) owes them free career training, or free college—or owes them a basic standard of living?

We should all remember that our **government does not produce any wealth.** Our government merely takes money away from those who work for a living, and then redistributes that money to someone else. On April 6, 2018, the *Wall Street Journal* reported that 20% of Americans pay 87% of all income taxes. Clearly, 80% of our population is becoming more and more dependent on our federal government to help sustain their daily lives.

Having made this observation, it is important to recognize that merely throwing money at social problems is not a good solution, unless the money results in fundamental changes in the way people live their lives, and results (if possible) in a more self-sustaining lifestyle for those folks who are the recipients of this help. I have worked directly with this type of problem and have seen the destructive nature of socialism. It destroys a person's sense of self-determination and self-responsibility. Even worse, it makes them dependent on Big Government. I compare this to being hooked on the very dangerous drug that I call **OPM**—*Other Peoples' Money*. It can be very destructive to human life.

And, what is true with humans is mirrored in the animal world. Adult animals teach their babies how to survive in the wild. However, they lose their skills and ability to survive once they become domesticated by humans and learn to depend on humans for their survival. That is why, in many states, it is against the law to capture various wild animals and try to turn them into pets.

Thomas Jefferson, the 3rd President of the United States, was a student of world history and is considered by many to be one of the most brilliant persons to have served in that position. Former President John F. Kennedy said that Thomas Jefferson was the most intelligent person to have ever been in the White House. A review of history suggests that President Kennedy's observation was very accurate.

Thomas Jefferson stated:

> *"Democracy will cease to exist when you take away from those who are willing to work and give to those who would not."*

In 1864, President Abraham Lincoln spoke about the good that our Free-Enterprise System provides to US citizens. *President Lincoln stated that our system allows and encourages all citizens to become wealthy—through their entrepreneurism and industrious work ethic.* He stated that "property" is the fruit of labor. Property is desirable; it is a positive good in the world. That some should be rich shows that others may become rich…."

In 1948 and 1945, another highly respected world leader by the name of **Winston Churchill** *stated*:

1. **"Socialism is the philosophy of failure** and the creed of ignorance..."

2. "The inherent virtue of **Socialism is the equal sharing of miseries."**

Unfortunately, today, many people fail to read or understand world history and why so many governments have failed with their **Socialistic systems that evolved into dictatorships—where citizens lost their freedoms and opportunities to improve the quality of their life.**

Venezuela is a perfect example for today's youth, concerning how socialism can ruin an economy and the lives of its citizens. Just a few decades ago, **Venezuela** was a very prosperous, entrepreneurial country and was the economic engine of South America. Then the people elected a Socialist, named Hugo Chavez, as their new President. He condemned the free-enterprise system and promised to redistribute the wealth by giving government handouts to everyone. The voters loved him and marched in the streets in support of his policies.

Then, President Chavez became a dictator and destroyed the country's economy, by nationalizing industry after industry, starting with the banks and then the petroleum industry. Today, citizens are leaving Venezuela as fast as they can—while many of the people who remain have to steal or beg for food, just to survive. Today, medical care is non-existent, and major crime is running rampant throughout the country. Chaos and riots now permeate this country. Is this going to be the future for America? I am very worried about this possibility.

Prior to that, in 1987, Robert Mugabe became the President of **Zimbabwe,** which was a wealthy country—described as the "bread-basket of Africa," and the most promising country on the continent (*NY Times*). Mugabe promised voters prosperity through Socialism and redistribution of the country's wealth. Zimbabwe soon became a dictatorship, its economy collapsed, and now Zimbabwe can't even feed its own citizens—let alone feed the other countries in Africa.

It now appears that the leadership of **South Africa** is pursuing the same Socialistic changes and redistribution of wealth that contributed to the downfall of Zimbabwe and Venezuela.

Dear readers, we need look no further than to our next-door neighbor, **Cuba,** to understand the economic devastation and loss of individual freedom that Socialism forces on its citizens. How many people do you see wanting to immigrate to Cuba—None! Instead, Cubans want to move to the United States.

In March of 2019, another economic bombshell was dropped on the world, when "the entire government of Finland resigned," because its working-age population can no longer support the social-welfare programs (including its Universal Basic Income Program) that were implemented in the past. Apparently, the current government does not have the guts or integrity to implement the welfare reforms that are necessary to return Finland to a financially stable and viable country. So, the elected officials are taking the coward's way out, and running away from the social problems they and their predecessors created—which will hurt all working citizens even more.

Considering the foregoing, why are so many Americans, especially today's youth, demanding that we follow the disastrous Socialistic Policies of these failed countries that are in economic ruin—where, in the end, everyone lost? If America turns Socialistic like these countries, today's youth will pay a very heavy financial price, and severely limit their ability to achieve the *"American Dream."* Remember, **today's youth will soon become tomorrow's "Working-Class,"** who will be heavily taxed, so that our government can give their money to other people!

Every future generation should have an opportunity to experience and live the "American Dream," by becoming highly successful entrepreneurs through their own Personal Strategic Planning. But, this cannot happen under a socialistic dictatorship—that kills the incentives needed by entrepreneurs to become successful. As stated earlier—*each of us is an entrepreneur in this life.*

Every US citizen should be concerned about our county's future and the rush toward Socialism by many politicians. **Remember, government does not create wealth or jobs. It merely takes the wealth away from those who work and create value for society and redistributes it to others—for its own purpose.** This usually results in a dictatorship that gains more and more power and control over the lives of its citizens.

In return, the citizens become poorer and poorer, have less freedom, and begin to live in fear of their heavy-handed government. Unfortunately, by the time the citizens realize the consequences of these Socialistic dictatorships—it is too late to regain control of their country and their lives. I sincerely hope that this is not a glimpse of America's future!

President Thomas Jefferson was spot-on with his assessment of big government, and the damage it can do—**if its citizens allow this to happen.**

As other world leaders such as President Abraham Lincoln and Winston Churchill also recognized, big Socialistic governments actually destroy the incentives and initiatives of its own citizens. In turn, these governments that were actually elected and controlled by its citizens—now control the very citizens who gave them their power. Why? Because the citizens allowed this to happen—foolishly believing that big government was going to level the playing field, redistribute the wealth, and make everybody happy. Again, just look at Cuba!

Please remember—Big Government does not owe you or me a living, nor does any corporation or small business. In Part III of this book, I relate how I achieved the "American Dream" without receiving any government aid or other free financial support. And, I started out without a dollar in my pocket when I left our small farm in Hoagland, Indiana, after graduating high school. Well, I might have had $1.00—but that was about it! On our farm, I had a younger brother who I used to call "Money-Bags." I think he might have accumulated at least $10.00 by the time he left our farm. Wow—he was rolling in the dough! ☺

Now, after experiencing the real world, I clearly understand that you and I have the greatest opportunity to achieve nearly any career that we might dream—if we are willing to discipline ourselves and pay the price needed to achieve that dream. Granted, there are some occupations that some of us will never achieve. After all, at my height, I had no possibility of playing the center position for an NBA basketball team. However, there are thousands of other careers that each of us can pursue in this Good Ole United States of America.

Therefore, we owe it to ourselves to develop and follow a Personal Strategic Plan that will steer us toward achievement of our own career goals and dreams.

Another important lesson I learned during my career is that *other people or businesses will richly reward us for helping them achieve their dreams*—as long as we do it more efficiently and better than anyone else. Again, it's about helping others improve their lives.

The fact that nobody owes you or me a living is one of the most important concepts that successful people and entrepreneurs clearly understand. You and I have every opportunity to achieve the "American Dream," so **go out and earn it!**

Foolish and lazy people turn to Socialism for their daily needs—not realizing that Socialism has ruined the lives of millions of people throughout the world.

Nobody Owes You or Me a Living—

Especially Big Government!

CHAPTER 10

A Good Reputation Is Invaluable

There are many pieces to this complex puzzle that shows us the secret of how to succeed and have a chance to live the "American Dream."

Besides our body and brain, our most important asset is our reputation.

Throughout my career, I was amazed and saddened by the number of people who would give their soul to the devil—if they thought it would advance their career or gain them an extra dollar or two.

We have all heard the old adage that "You can fool some of the people some of the time, but you can't fool all of the people all of the time." Yet, some people continue to believe they can lie, cheat, or walk over other people to get ahead, and that their actions will never catch up with them.

Not surprisingly, I found this destructive quality exists in people regardless of their age or level of education, and regardless of where they went to college.

What these folks fail to realize is that most people with whom they associate already know that they are not to be trusted. Over time, this kind of flawed reputation will have an impact on the perpetrator and will negatively impact their career potential and achievements. This flaw can be very costly!

I was raised in a family where, if we lied, we got our butts spanked—with a belt. Therefore, being honest and forthright was the second good quality (beyond hard work) that our dad instilled into each of his children.

Being honest has many benefits. First, we have a clear conscience and feel good about ourselves. Second, it is much easier to be truthful than to try to cover up a lie. These factors alone give honest people a huge advantage during their careers and in their personal lives.

On the other hand, I should also point out that being honest will not always result in good things happening to us. Why? Because, it provides dishonest people with insights into to how they can use us for their benefit, or stab us in the back to enhance their career. I will discuss this in greater detail in Part III.

It is good to remember that our life is a journey, not a short sprint. For all of us, there will be disappointments and set-backs along the way. But, over time, people who retain their honesty, values, morals and good work ethic will usually win, and come out on top.

The best proof I have for you is my personal experience, which is contained in Part III of this book: "My Life As An Entrepreneur—A Road Less Traveled."

A Good Reputation is Invaluable. Please—never lose your Good Reputation!

Protect Your Good Reputation

Advanced Education Is Important

Politicians love to play the "Envy Game" and point out how unfair it is for successful people to have much more in economic worth than those who are labeled to be among the "Have Not's."

Well, many if not **most of those who have a great deal of wealth did not inherit their net worth**, nor did they get it from the government. **They got it the hard way—they earned it,** just like the "Heroes" in my life! Presidents Jefferson and Lincoln would have been proud of these hard-working entrepreneurs.

During childhood, one of my English teachers loved to read poetry. One of her favorite quotes was from Emily Dickinson's 1873 letter, in which she wrote "There is no Frigate like a Book." This letter became one of Ms. Dickinson's most famous poems—because it describes how a person can mentally sail (travel) anywhere while reading a book. This phrase is also a wonderful way of expressing our career opportunities in life, through reading and learning.

By gaining knowledge through advanced training and education, each of us has an opportunity to travel to the wonderful world of success and rise above any level of poverty, bullying, or other negative influences we might experience in our life. Post-high school education was the Great Equalizer in my life. Remember, "There is no Frigate like a Book," and *higher education was the "Frigate" to my professional success, and for the many heroes I met during my career. It can also be your road to prosperity. The choice is up to you*, and no one else—*No Excuses!*

It is very important for every student to realize that their *advanced training or college is their first job after graduating high school. Really, a job? Yes, a job!*

Let me explain. The quality of education we achieve from our advanced training or college will impact our career opportunities immediately when we, as members of our graduating class, interview for job openings.

The interviewing process is the first time that many graduates wake up to the reality that the quality of their schoolwork (and the major they chose) will be key factors that determine which important employers will grant them an interview.

So, beware of the social life of parties, parties, and more parties while pursuing an education beyond high school. Yes, parties might be a lot of fun. Just make sure they don't become a priority in your life—because you are there to get an education that will allow you to become more valuable to others and to obtain your dream job upon graduation. Failure to make the most of your advanced training or college education could have a very detrimental impact on the rest of your life and your ability to achieve the "American Dream."

Remember, *advanced education is your first job after high school graduation*. This education will establish the skills that society and employers will want—or won't want. *It will establish the foundation for your economic future.*

Having said this, let me explain a bit further why advanced education beyond high school is so important. Recently, Intuit reported that "independent contractors" make up approximately 40% of the entire US workforce and are expected to account for 43% of the US workforce by the year 2020.

Independent contractors are essentially entrepreneurs or self-employed people. This huge portion of the population will survive economically only if they provide a skill or value that others want and are willing to purchase. This fact further demonstrates that each of us is an entrepreneur, and each of us must develop our own base of knowledge and skills that others will hire for their benefit.

Now, some people believe that going to an expensive, high-profile college is needed for a person to succeed in life. This is not true!

Yes, choosing a college or university with a good reputation is important. But, I couldn't afford to go to an expensive, high-profile college. Besides, with the low scores on my college entrance exams, I would never have been admitted to those prestigious institutions. As a result, I enrolled at Ball State University in Muncie, Indiana, during an era when state-supported universities were required to accept nearly anyone who had a diploma from an Indiana high school.

My choice of selecting Ball State was a very positive turning point in my life. I found that I received an excellent education, and that major employers were eager to hire graduates from Ball State's College of Business.

I began college on academic probation but graduated with honors—at the top of the business college, while working multiple jobs to pay for my education. I did not receive any financial assistance or loans.

My wife chose Indiana State University for her college education. She also received an excellent education in the male-dominated field of Print Management, with a minor in business. Her college education was a very positive turning point in her life. During her career, she was named one of the Top 10 Business Women in the United States, by *Printing Impressions Magazine.*

During my career, I have had graduates from Harvard, Dartmouth, Princeton, MIT, Yale, and other high-profile universities reporting to me. I found that the quality of education I received at Ball State was excellent and prepared me very well to manage and lead graduates from these other educational institutions.

The bottom line is that few of us can qualify or afford to attend an expensive, high-profile college or university. The good news is that attending a lower-cost college or university does not put you or me at a disadvantage. Our career success largely depends on how seriously we pursue our education, then our career, and how we pursue continuing education throughout our career.

So, what is your "Personal Strategic Plan" for advanced training or college beyond high school? If you don't have one, please start your plan today.

Advanced Education Is Essential

So, Let's Board Our Education Frigate

CHAPTER 12

Learning Is a Lifelong Process

The environment in which we live today is vastly different from that of my childhood, when nearly everything we purchased was made in the good ole USA. We now live in a world economy and compete for education and jobs with people throughout the world—from China, to India, to Europe, etc.

In addition, technology is advancing at the fastest pace our world has ever experienced. Many high school graduates from prior decades didn't understand this reality, and many of them found their jobs outsourced to foreign countries during their careers or replaced by robots or other advanced technologies. Unfortunately, with little or no education beyond high school, many of those folks found it very difficult to maintain employment or financial stability throughout their lives. ***They became technologically obsolete!***

Generations of high school graduates experienced this phenomenon—not just the Statler Brothers' "Class of '57." The rapid changes that are taking place with technology today are forcing bigger and bigger changes in our society and in people's careers. But, in doing so, these changes are also creating new and exciting opportunities for those who have a good education beyond high school, and for those who seize the opportunity to embrace change.

Advancements in technology have made our lives better in many respects, while causing increased pressure on each of us to keep pace with these changes. This is why we must make learning a lifelong process.

It is estimated that there has been more new technology developed during the past 100 years than throughout all of human history, and that (overall) new technology is doubling approximately every 5 years—with computers doubling their capacities every 12–18 months.

I clearly remember the telephone we had at our farmhouse. It was a wooden box that was screwed onto our kitchen wall. We were on a "party line," which meant that at least three families shared our telephone line and could listen to any call we received. To make a call, we had to turn a hand-crank. We knew when we had an incoming call because the bell on our phone would ring as two short rings and one long ring.

In my childhood days, computers did not exist. Today, our personal cell phones are so advanced that they also serve as powerful computers—something we could not have dreamed of just a decade or so ago. With the accelerated pace of advances in technology, we can only speculate how our lives will change during the next 25 years. But, we know it will be significant.

I found that continuing education throughout my career was an important factor that contributed to my success. Beyond a business degree, I took courses in graduate law, computer science, manufacturing processes, quality control, etc. I continually searched for knowledge that could help me improve or reinvent myself and my various businesses.

As a result of this broader education, I was able to hold intelligent conversations with physicists, scientists, engineers, inventors, and others. Those conversations frequently led to re-envisioning how I approached business problems that needed to be solved—and greatly helped me revitalize and rebuild my struggling companies.

It will be nearly impossible for anyone to achieve and maintain the "American Dream" from this time forward unless they incorporate continuing education into their lives. Please, don't look at this as a burden, because continuing education is a golden opportunity for today's youth who wish to achieve the "American Dream."

To me, continuing education was not an option—but a necessity. It will surely be a necessity for today's youth. And, it can be a very enjoyable process.

Otherwise, today's younger generation will quickly become obsolete in their careers, because a lack of knowledge regarding advancing technologies will prevent them from incorporating important new considerations into their everyday leadership and decision-making processes. Those folks who do not pursue continuing education or technical training will eventually be surpassed in their careers by people who remain current with new and emerging technologies.

Part III of this book contains many examples of how continuing education helped me achieve success. Conversely, when I owned a high-tech print-communications company, 75% of all of my competitors went out of business—because they failed to keep pace with emerging technologies.

Our Education Should Never Stop

CHAPTER 13

First Job After College

The first job a person takes after graduating college is one of the most, if not the most important career decision they will ever make—beyond choosing their advanced training or college education.

Many graduates want to move back home, get a job with a big company, and work in a cozy team environment, where decisions are made by consensus. What a safe decision! Doesn't that give you a warm and fuzzy feeling? Well, to me this was not entrepreneurism, nor was this approach an opportunity for self-determination or professional growth.

I received multiple job offers. Some were excellent opportunities, including returning to my former employer, Marathon Oil Company. However, had I done so, I would have become "a little spoke in a giant wheel," at their corporate headquarters in Findlay, Ohio.

Yes, this would have been a comfortable move with a wonderful company, but returning to a giant company would not have provided the challenging environment I wanted—nor would it have provided the accelerated learning experience that I was about to receive.

For me, it was important that my first job provide an opportunity to rise to a new level of achievement, by applying my college education to the fullest extent possible. This is exactly what I achieved by taking a position at a newly established office of an international CPA firm.

This position allowed me to apply my college education into the real world of manufacturing, insurance, banking, wholesale distribution, government audits, financial reporting, taxation, and consulting.

In addition, I received extensive summer training that helped raise my education and career to a level that I could not have experienced anywhere else. During this time, I also studied business law in the MBA program at Indiana University, which proved to be an invaluable asset throughout my career.

So, every graduate should give careful consideration concerning how their first job out of college will provide them with an opportunity to leverage their education and propel them into a promising career.

In Part III of this book, I discuss a conversation that I had with a US Senator's aide who failed to understand the importance of making a wise decision when she chose her first job after graduating college. She chose to pursue what appeared to be a glamorous job working for one of her US Senators in Washington, D.C., rather than building on the expertise that she had learned with her college major.

Her decision greatly changed her life—and not for the better, as you will soon read.

After College—Choose Your First Job Wisely

CHAPTER 14

Starting at the Bottom

Our time on this Earth is short, but it seems like a long learning process, especially during our youthful days. In truth, we all start at the bottom of the knowledge scale—and we continue to learn throughout our career. This is good, because starting at the bottom gives us an opportunity to gain the experience and confidence we need to climb the ladder of success, in our pursuit of the "American Dream."

This reminds me of the story about an upstart college graduate from a prestigious university, who visited with the proverbial Great Guru at the top of a mountain. The new graduate said, "Great Guru, I just graduated with my MBA from Big-Time University, and I want to achieve great success. How do I achieve great success?" The Guru responded, "Make good decisions, my boy; make good decisions." To which the graduate stated, "How do I know if I'm making good decisions?" The Guru responded, "Experience, my boy; from experience." The graduate then asked, "How do I get experience, Great Guru?" The Guru responded, "By making mistakes, my boy—by making mistakes."

As Frank Sinatra sang: "That's Life." Yes, that's life. We all make mistakes along the way. These are learning experiences that teach us lessons, so that we (hopefully) will not make the same mistake again and again.

Renowned scientist Albert Einstein found great joy when one of his experiments failed—because each failure gave Mr. Einstein an opportunity to learn something new and gain experiences that he otherwise would not have had.

All of us start at the bottom, and all of us learn from our experiences—sometimes from the mistakes that we make and sometimes from mistakes that we see others make. Either way, mistakes give us learning opportunities.

Hopefully, we learn from our mistakes and apply our newly acquired knowledge toward making better decisions in the future.

Although I started at the bottom, I now understand that I had a huge advantage over many of my peers. You see, my dad worked our butts off on the farm. We got punished if we did not get our farm chores done. Therefore, we learned how to work very hard and get our chores completed every day, and on time. Learning to be disciplined and to fulfill our responsibilities and be responsible for our actions are values that each of us need to have, if we hope to succeed in the real world.

Few of my peers or today's youth experience or learn this type of discipline—which provides those who are dedicated and disciplined with a huge advantage, as they strive to achieve the "American Dream."

In fact, I would suggest that *the opportunities to achieve the "American Dream" are more abundant today than when I grew up*—because today there are fewer people willing to make the commitments and sacrifices that are necessary to succeed at this level. What is your level of commitment? *Think about it!*

As I look back over my life, I now have a better understanding concerning why nearly all of the highly successful people I met along the way started at the bottom. It was their dedication and struggle that helped them reach the top of their professional careers. In retrospect, these were the lucky folks!

As discussed later in this book, my friend Harold McMaster started with nothing. Despite his physical disabilities, Harold became an outstanding scientist, inventor, and entrepreneur. In the next chapter, I will discuss several other people, including my wife, Angel, who started at the bottom and achieved national greatness. These people are my heroes. I hope you find similar heroes in your life—and *I hope that you will become a hero to future generations.*

As further evidence that *starting at the bottom is an advantage*, during my career, I never met a highly successful person who was raised in a pampered lifestyle or who was born with a "silver spoon" in their mouth.

Our life cycle requires that each of us start at the bottom of the knowledge scale. The learning process establishes the discipline we need to make intelligent decisions as we strive to overcome the challenges and adversities that will confront us in this life. Therefore—

Starting at the Bottom Is Not a Disadvantage

Use It to Your Advantage!

CHAPTER 15

Success Requires
Struggle and Dedication

If success was easy, everyone would be successful.

During my career, the majority of failing businesses that I turned around and rebuilt were owned by 2nd- or 3rd-generation family members. These businesses were failing mainly because the current family members had little or no appreciation for the struggle and dedication their fathers or grandfathers experienced when building their successful businesses.

These spoiled brats (my perception) wanted the family business to continue to provide them with the luxurious lifestyle in which they were raised. Most had graduated from prestigious universities and were considered well educated.

However, they failed to realize that the world did not revolve around them—and that their only value to the world was what they, as owners, could do to improve the lives of their customers. In addition, I found these generational owners to be less than kind to their employees, who many treated with a lack of appreciation and respect—as though the employees were their servants.

Along with Harold McMaster, there are three other people whom I greatly admired during my career. Each achieved a high level of success by overcoming their very limited financial situation and by overcoming major obstacles in their lives. I call them my "American Heroes."

I greatly admire Dr. Ben Carson, the 2017 Presidential Appointee to head the US Department of Housing and Urban Development. Mr. Carson was raised in poverty by a single mother with a 3rd-grade education, in the inner-city of Detroit, where drug use and gang violence were common.

Despite this environment, with guidance from his mother, Mr. Carson became a highly acclaimed physician and Director of Pediatric Neurosurgery at the Johns Hopkins Children's Center—a position to which he was appointed when he was just 33 years old.

Wow! This man was committed to overcoming his disadvantaged childhood and was determined not to become a "victim" of his environment. Instead, he overcame huge obstacles and achieved the "American Dream." Every young adult who experiences poverty should aspire to achieve this level of success. To me, Dr. Ben Carson is a true American Hero.

The next person I greatly admire is Dr. Phil, from the *Dr. Phil* TV show. Phillip C. McGraw had every right to end up on the trash heap of life. He was raised in a dysfunctional family with an alcoholic father and lived through a childhood of poverty. Instead of falling into his father's dysfunctional lifestyle, through pure struggle and dedication, Phillip C. McGraw earned his doctoral degree in clinical psychology in 1979. Eventually, he became a litigation consultant and now has his own very successful TV show—where he devotes his life to helping other people improve their lives. What an honorable mission!

Dr. Phil (as he puts it) "Got Real" with his life, learned from the past, and was determined to take control of his future—regardless of the price he would have to pay and the struggles he would have to endure. He took control over the 80–90% of the factors in his life that he could control. And so can you!

Dr. Phil achieved the "American Dream." To me, he is an American Hero.

The most important person I admire is my wife, Angel, who, like me, came from a small town and from a family that had no history of education beyond high school. Despite her small-town upbringing and no money, my wife worked her way through college as a waitress, without scholarships or grants—and paid for every dime of her education, while earning a degree in the male-dominated field of Print Management.

Angel was with me every step of the way, while rebuilding the insolvent printing company that we ended up owning. On the day we entered this company, it had no money to make its payroll and was more than $2.5 million in debt for obsolete equipment the owner had purchased. Its two banks were demanding that the company repay all of its loans—and potential customers did not want to work with the company because of its poor quality and broken promises in the past. As an old sailor might say, "This company was taking on water faster than a sinking ship."

During the next 15 years, Angel and I paid off every creditor and rebuilt our company from a low-quality, commodity printer—into one of the most respected high-tech print-communications companies in the United States, serving the education, plastics, and packaging markets.

By the time we retired, we had the finest reputation in the marketplace and were a primary supplier to nearly all of the major education publishers—including The National Geographic Society, whose VP of Global Procurement contacted my wife to see if we would be willing to become their partner in the supply of high-quality print materials.

Wow, what an honor to have a firm that was considered to be the top-quality publisher in the world contact us to establish a business partnership! And yes, we did become a key supplier for their high-quality print materials.

As a side note, National Geographic Society honored our firm by requesting that we become their partner in producing "The Lost Gospel" and "The Gospel of Judas Iscariot," which was a top-secret project until the books were released.

During our ownership, Angel was featured as one of the Top 10 Women Business Entrepreneurs in America by *Printing Impressions Magazine.*

To me, Harold McMaster, Dr. Carson, Dr. Phil, and my wife, Angel, all represent the best of America—and all are my American Heroes.

Now, some readers might think that my wife and I had a great ride down easy street when rebuilding this printing company, right? Well, there is no such thing as a ride down easy street. Struggle and dedication are behind the success of most entrepreneurs. We all pay a price for our success and achievements.

My wife and I paid a very heavy price for our success, because during those 15 years of our ownership, we did not take a single week of vacation. We worked seven days a week, up to 18 hours a day—and I suffered my first heart attack. There will be more about struggle and dedication in Part III of this book.

Several years ago, I listened to a nationally recognized college professor who teaches one of the top entrepreneur programs in the United States. During his talk, he stated that he had conducted experiments that had proven that entrepreneurs are not "gamblers." He proved this theory by sending a handful of entrepreneurs to Las Vegas with gambling money. Few of those people gambled with their money. Therefore, he concluded that entrepreneurs are not gamblers.

Well, this professor was correct to state that entrepreneurs are not foolish people who "gamble" with their money. But, successful entrepreneurs must take calculated risks when building their businesses, because it is only by taking risks and making changes that entrepreneurs are able to stay ahead of their competition. Taking no risks will lead to failure—just ask the many business owners who go out of business each year.

So, the key point is not that entrepreneurs are not gamblers. The key point is that all successful entrepreneurs take calculated risks, to which they have given a great deal of study and thought. However, when doing so, the entrepreneur must also face the consequences when his decisions don't result in success. This is the type of dedication and struggle that entrepreneurs must face every day.

Nothing exemplifies the important contribution that struggle and dedication contribute toward success than the metamorphosis of a pupa into a butterfly, which I call "the birth of a butterfly."

While in its cocoon, the pupa goes through a metamorphosis, during which it struggles mightily to transform itself into a butterfly. It would appear that this is a cruel process for this creature to endure. So, wouldn't it be a kind gesture for someone to help the butterfly just a bit, by opening the cocoon and letting the butterfly out, so it can begin enjoying life—and we can enjoy its beauty?

Well folks, bad news! If we tamper with nature's life-cycle and help the butterfly escape, the pupa will fall helplessly to the ground and die. Why? It is because nature requires the pupa to endure a struggle to transfer and transform its body mass into the beautiful butterfly that we eventually see.

And so it is with humans—it is our struggle and dedication through multiple challenges and obstacles in our lives that give us the strength and experience we need to succeed and achieve the "American Dream."

My Heroes: Harold McMaster, Dr. Ben Carson, Dr. Phil, and my wife, Angel all—

Became a Beautiful Butterfly

You, Too, Can Become a Beautiful Butterfly

CHAPTER 16

Money and Happiness

A nyone who thinks money will buy them happiness has a misconception of how money and happiness impact our lives. Just ask Ole Scrooge—who was never happy, no matter how much wealth he controlled.

I'll bet that most readers have met someone like Ole Scrooge in their life. Do you really want to be like him? Not me. I would rather be happy—and money, by itself, will not provide us with happiness!

Yes, money is a comforting factor that allows us to live our life in a sustainable manner. However, beyond that point, more money does not buy more happiness, unless we find a way to improve the lives of others by helping them become self-sufficient and prosperous in their own lives.

In regard to the importance of money, I am reminded of one of the world's wealthiest men, Warren Buffett, who could build or buy any mansion that he might desire. Yet, he and his wife continue to live in the home they purchased in 1958 for $31,000.

This home makes them happy—far more than living in a fancy mansion somewhere else.

Then, there was Sam Walton, the entrepreneur who started Wal-Mart and Sam's Club. Despite his vast wealth, Sam continued to drive his old pickup truck to and from work. This is what made Sam Walton happy—not spending money on himself. Instead, he used his wealth to create jobs for tens of thousands of people, nationwide.

I understand the priorities of Mr. Buffett and Mr. Walton. Instead of becoming "pigs at the trough," as we say on the farm, they did not live the self-indulging, free-spending lifestyle that we have seen with many people who became overnight celebrities. Neither of these highly successful entrepreneurs spent their wealth foolishly. As I have said before, being poor at a young age and *working hard for your wealth is not a disadvantage. It is an advantage*—as exemplified by these two successful entrepreneurs.

I, too, drive an older pickup truck. It gets me where I want to go and is needed to support our animal shelter in Brown County, Indiana, and to supply food for needy pets in our area. I am happy with my values and with helping others—including abused and abandoned puppy dogs and kitties. *Angel and I love their kisses.* ☺

By the way, if you want to get a good feel for the values and morals of most adults—observe how they treat their pets. People who fail to properly care for or abuse their pets will, in all probability, treat their fellow human beings in a similar manner.

Having come from a poor childhood environment, as a business entrepreneur, I was prudent and chose to re-invest all profits back into new equipment, new processes, and new technology. This benefited others by creating new and better-paying jobs that supported additional families. This is what happiness is all about. It is about helping others—and not being "pigs at the trough."

As a side note, not only did I put all profits back into creating new jobs, but as president, I made sure that I was one of the lowest-paid people in my company. Some of our employees made more than twice my salary. I know that as a company president I did things much differently than the "pigs at the trough" we hear about in the news. But remember—money does not buy happiness! Both you and I could rattle off a list of very wealthy people, including politicians, who lead miserable and unhappy lives. Don't end up like those folks!

And, think about this: When our life on this planet is over, who, if any of us, will be taking their Earthly treasures with them into their next life, in the Spirit World? Not me. In fact, I know of no one who has ever been successful in doing so—not even the great pharaohs of Egypt. I visited their tombs, and guess what—the treasures that were buried with them are still there or are in the national museum in Cairo. So, what was the purpose of amassing this vast wealth—was it merely to support their huge egos? After all, it doesn't do them any good today! And, of what value is their Earthly ego to them in the After-Life?

Last, if anyone thinks that money will buy them happiness—just look at how winning the lottery ruined the lives of many people. Some are already financially broke, while others are no longer alive.

Over time, I believe that most adults realize that money is not the source of our happiness here on Earth. It is a necessity for our daily lives—but it is not the Holy Grail for achieving happiness. Happiness comes from within our souls and the knowledge that we are doing our best—while helping others rise to a higher level, so they, too, can achieve the goals in their life, including the "American Dream."

Money Does Not Buy Happiness

CHAPTER 17

Never Go into Business to Get Rich

Earlier, I stated that each of us is an entrepreneur. We have our God-given body and brain. What we do with these assets is 80–90% within our control. We are the CEO of our own lives and have more control over our future than everyone else combined.

Each year, when mentoring high school or college students who are studying entrepreneurship or career planning, I ask the students how many want to go into business and get rich. Next, I ask them how many want to go into business so they can be their own boss. Usually, the majority of students in each class will raise their hands in the affirmative regarding both questions.

Well, those probably would have been my answers years ago, if I had studied career planning or entrepreneurship in school. But then—the real world taught me a secret of how entrepreneurs succeed!

First, *nobody wants to make you or me rich! The rest of the world wants you and me to take actions that will make their lives better.* People care about themselves first, not about making you or me rich! Who are we trying to kid with our selfish thinking? We are only fooling ourselves!

This is a lesson many failing entrepreneurs (business owners and employees) do not understand. *It is when we make the lives of others better that they will reward us* with more of their business or with promotions and financial raises. *This is the Holy Grail for a successful career.*

Second, successful entrepreneurs, who are business owners, have many bosses. They are accountable to and report to all of their customers, their employees, their suppliers, their bankers, etc. When a person is a business owner, that entrepreneur has many people they must keep happy and many people they must treat well, or those folks will take their business or employment skills somewhere else.

The foregoing are "Truths" that many 2nd- and 3rd-generation family owners never learn—and that is why so many of them end up failing when they take over a business from their parents or grandparents. They continue to think that the world revolves around them and that their customers and employees exist to serve their needs and make them happy. What Fools!

In reality, each of us is an entrepreneur, and none of us will truly be our own boss. Instead, like business owners, we will have many bosses—all of whom must be kept happy, or we will lose their support, and we will fail to achieve our full potential.

Whether we are entrepreneurial business owners or employees, there is no guaranteed path to wealth. Each of us has an opportunity to excel at a higher level than any of our competitors—with the hope that those in charge (our customers or our bosses) will recognize our outstanding contributions and reward us accordingly. Please remember—

Nobody Wants to Make You or Me Rich

We Must Earn Our Success

CHAPTER 18

Excuses

I love to hate this topic. It's similar to playing the "Victim" role. No one wins!

Anyone can make excuses for their lack of achievement. There probably isn't an excuse that exists today that someone didn't use decades or centuries ago—except that, in today's world, a student can claim that they lost their homework because their computer crashed! When I was a youngster, computers didn't exist. Instead, we blamed our family dog for eating or destroying our homework! *(Dear Brownie, you were such a good puppy dog. I'm glad I never blamed you for my poor performance in high school. I earned all of my bad grades without any help. No Excuses from me!)*

In my opinion, using an excuse is a crippling human condition. Excuses are a way to rationalize in our minds a justification to explain our lack of success in whatever we are doing. It means that the person making the excuse has given up on success, rather than try to figure out how to get back on track and achieve the goals that will lead to improvement in their life.

I remember going back to several of my high school reunions. In hindsight, they truly were a mirror image of the Statler Brothers' song, "The Class of '57."

Many classmates never left the local area, and few pursued training or education beyond high school. Yet, many of them had excuses for their situation in life. It seemed that their most important goal was to get a job and get married. Some girls got pregnant, or got married and then got pregnant, and stayed home to raise their kids. Some of the guys lost their factory jobs when their companies shut down or moved away. Many of these "victims" blamed someone else for their situation in life, but did little to make themselves more valuable to society.

Very few classmates saw themselves as entrepreneurs, in charge of their own life. *Many let life happen "To Them," instead of making life happen "For Them."* Or, they thought that belonging to a big labor union would make their jobs secure—which they found out was not true, when their companies shut down or moved away from the local area.

Anyone can make excuses. Don't be one of those people. Don't be a victim! You are in control of your future, so put together a Personal Strategic Plan, and dedicate your life toward achieving success in whatever you do.

No Excuses!

CHAPTER 19

Lack of Money

A lack of money is not a valid reason for failure. Look at the success of Harold McMaster, Dr. Ben Carson, Dr. Phil, and my wife. They all started with nothing.

When I left the farm, I was very poor. So, I worked two jobs to get enough money to further my education. First, I peeled potatoes at a McDonald's restaurant and then went to a Firestone Store, where I was a tire changer and a grease monkey. Yes, during my youth, we really did peel potatoes to make fries at McDonald's.

I didn't go out and party or spend money on a new automobile like some of my classmates. *I didn't get married or make babies—nor should you, if you want to improve your chances for economic success in life.*

When I returned to Ball State University, I did so with only $1,000 in the bank. In those days, I did not qualify for academic scholarships, government grants, or loans to help finance my education. Yet, I never considered myself a "victim," and I didn't try to make "excuses" for not proceeding with my college education.

Instead, I got tough with myself and worked my way through Ball State by managing a 17-unit apartment complex where I was also the janitor, painter, plumber, and handyman. I also earned money by working as a grease monkey at a local Marathon Gas Station, and by joining the US Army Reserves. I kept those jobs while maintaining a full academic schedule. This was not an easy time in my life, but I was determined to succeed, despite my "Lack of Money."

Later in the business world, I learned that, if a leader has a proven record of success, there is always a financial institution that will lend them money. I have taken over failing companies that had millions of dollars of debt and yet was able to get financing to keep those businesses alive, thus giving me time to find the problems and make the changes that were needed to rebuild the failing company. I discuss this topic extensively in Part III of this book.

Then, I made sure that *every creditor got repaid every dime* that they were owed. Remember, "A Good Reputation Is Invaluable!" But—

A Lack of Money Is Not an Excuse for Failure

CHAPTER 20

Never Quit on Yourself

If you don't believe in yourself—who will?

If I had listened to my dad and my high school counselor, I never would have left the local area, obtained further education, or challenged myself to succeed.

The truth is—*People fail only when they quit on themselves.* So, another key to success is *"Don't Quit on Yourself!"*

Remember, you and I are independent entrepreneurs. We are the CEOs of our own lives, and we control 80–90% of what will happen to us. *Make life happen "For You." Don't let life happen "To You"! You, and only you, are in control. No excuses!*

So, despite the obstacles and challenges hurled at us during our life—each of us must continue to pursue our "American Dream" by unwaveringly sticking to our Personal Strategic Plan, or by adjusting it so we can get back on track and achieve our goals. Again, if you don't already have a PSP, please begin developing one as soon as possible. *Be comforted by the fact that you are regaining control of your life—or are gaining control of your life for the first time. Think about it—isn't this a wonderful and empowering feeling?* ☺

None of us will ever be perfect, and all of us will stumble and fall along the way. The Good Lord knows that I have! But, each time I fell or got knocked down, I got back up on my feet and struggled even harder to achieve my goals.

Please remember—no one fails when they stumble. We learn from our setbacks. Then, we get back into the game and continue pursuing our "American Dream."

As mentioned earlier, I love the attitude of scientist Albert Einstein. Einstein loved his failed experiments, because it was from the failed experiments that he learned something new. *Learn from Albert Einstein: never quit on yourself.*

And so it is with our lives. If we succeeded every time we tried something new, we would lose the opportunity to learn from our setbacks. As the Great Guru stated, we gain experience by learning from our mistakes. This is a great lesson—learn from your setbacks, but *never stop pursuing your dreams.*

In this regard, I must confess that I loved the mindset of NFL Hall of Fame coach Vince Lombardi. When looking for players to add to his team, the #1 quality the coach looked for was the player who could take a hit, get back up on his feet, and get back in the game. He didn't look for the most gifted athlete, although some of his players were very gifted. Instead, he chose those players who were committed to playing the entire game, and those players who would not quit on themselves. Those of us who succeed will stay in the game and give it every effort we have, until we achieve success—not in a Super Bowl, but in pursuit of our "American Dream."

Some of us might not believe that we are the most gifted people on this Earth. The Good Lord knows that I didn't think that I was highly gifted! But, that doesn't mean that we can't achieve incredible results with the talents we have.

After reading Part III, you will understand the disadvantages I faced in my life, the many struggles I experienced, and the challenges I faced throughout my career. I was a Vince Lombardi type of player. I got knocked down many times, but got back on my feet every time—and got back into this game we call life!

It would have been very easy for me to play the "Victim" role, or create "Excuses," or give up and fail because of a "Lack of Money." But, I never gave up or quit on myself—and *you should "Never Quit on yourself" while pursuing your "American Dream."*

Harold McMaster, Dr. Carson, Dr. Phil, and my wife, Angel—

Never Quit on Themselves

And Neither Should You

CHAPTER 21

Friends, Friends, Mentors, and Friends

The term **"Friend"** has different meanings to different people, and it changes—because we have many different kinds of friends during our lives. All of them are important and affect us differently, in many ways.

First, there are the **"friends" with whom we go to school,** whether it is high school, vocational school, or college. If you are in college and hang around with other students who are majoring in your field, you probably call them your "friends." Although there is a degree of truth in this, you should also realize that some of those friends are also your competitors. *Really,* you ask? Yes, *really.*

Why would I make such a statement? It's very simple. While in career training or college, we are competing with every student in our class who is pursuing a similar major in their degree program, because all of us want to achieve the best grades possible and graduate in the upper tier of our class. Otherwise, why would any college or university spend so much time with testing and grading students—and why would potential employers care about a student's grades?

Then, when interviewing for career positions during our last semester, each of us will be competing with everyone else who is interviewing for those same job openings. Every graduating senior will want to get offers from the best firms, for the best positions. However, not everyone will be granted an interview or be extended a job offer for those positions. Our student grade point average and academic standing will be among the important factors that employers will consider during their hiring process.

Friendships that we gain through education seldom last beyond graduation, unless, by coincidence, several of you end up working at the same firm or in the same community. Even then, those friendships usually do not last.

Next, there are our co-workers who we call "friends." Generally, these bonds are stronger than the friendships we had during our educational process. Why? I think it is because co-workers share similar goals and challenges; therefore, to a greater degree, they need and rely on each other for support in the organization they work for and from which they receive their paychecks.

However, once you or I leave that place of employment, most, if not all, of those friendships will vanish—if not immediately, then within a year. Why? It is because we are no longer working with and no longer share similar goals and challenges with our former co-workers. In other words, we are no longer of significant value to them—unless they can use us as part of their network to improve their future career opportunities elsewhere.

The reality is that, after leaving a place of employment, former co-workers re-focus their attention toward those people who remain and can help them continue to achieve their career goals, in pursuit of their "American Dream."

The best way to explain the loss of friendships after leaving a place of employment is to compare this experience to one of our favorite pastimes—eating. When we leave a place of employment, we become no more valuable or desirable to those we leave behind than the stale bagels that are left over from yesterday's breakfast buffet. I've been there and experienced it, multiple times.

It doesn't matter whether we leave to pursue better opportunities or whether we involuntarily lose our job. Either way, the person leaving becomes similar to yesterday's stale bagel that most former co-workers no longer want—unless they can use you or me to advance their own careers. I can assure you that it's no fun when you realize that you are "yesterday's stale bagel."

As Mr. Wonderful on *Shark Tank* says: "Life is tough!" He is humorously correct—although when we experience it, it isn't very funny!

Career Mentors are a third group of "friends" that (sadly) *many people overlook.* These are the highly skilled people who can help us grow, both personally and in our careers. These are the well-educated professionals who have achieved success in other careers or in other industries. *These are some of the most important "friends" we will ever have in life,* because their knowledge, counsel, and guidance can literally change our lives—for the better. This group of friends contributed immensely to my professional success—and I thank them greatly for their friendship and contributions. In turn, I helped many of these friends become more successful in their careers. It is important that these friendships are not one-sided, but provide a benefit to both parties.

Each time I assumed the presidency of a failing company, I surrounded myself with scientists, engineers, computer specialists, and other experts from outside my company, who were not financial people, like me. These were people who broadened my decision-making processes by giving me technical insights into how I could do a better job of formulating the strategies that were needed to rebuild my failing company.

Why did I need these outsiders? The answer is clear. If the failing company already had a strong and knowledgeable management team, the company wouldn't need me—because it wouldn't be failing. Instead, it would be a successful and prospering company, and I wouldn't have been hired as the new president to come in and save the company from financial ruin.

Therefore, since I have a strong financial and manufacturing background, I surrounded myself with "Career Mentors" who could make me a more complete leader, with advice they could provide from their diverse backgrounds. I joined engineering clubs and venture-capital organizations, where I could expand my network of people who had these diverse, technical backgrounds.

Understandably, these folks might not have been knowledgeable about my needs, but over time, through one-on-one conversations, I found ways to work with many of them to reshape my company into an innovative industry leader.

It is truly amazing how much we can learn from the knowledge and experiences of other experts and find ways to apply newly gained knowledge into our own business situation. These people provided a tremendous boost to my career—without realizing the valuable contributions they were making. Best of all, we had wonderful conversations when we challenged each other and tested each other's thinking—all with the knowledge that we weren't competing with each other in our professional careers. These were truly enriching and rewarding experiences that I will never forget. *Everyone benefited from these conversations, and that is a key to building successful mentor relationships.*

I'm sure everyone has heard the old adage that "Birds of a feather flock together." Please don't become one of the "Birds of a feather who flock together." Instead, soar with the eagles, and broaden your knowledge base by learning from people with different educational disciplines, careers, and ethnic backgrounds. It is my hope that every reader of this book will find terrific "Career Mentors" in their life—as I did during my career.

Unfortunately, as everyone moves on with their career, many of these excellent mentor relationships gradually come to an end—but they were wonderful while they lasted. This is a good example of why I am so happy that I was raised in an environment that hammered home the fact that I was not the "Smartest Guy in the Room." You will read about some of my terrific "Career Mentors" in Part III of this book.

Now, we come to "personal friends." These folks have nothing to do with our business or profession—although one or two might have worked with us in the past. In any event, these are the people who will stick with us no matter what circumstances impact our lives.

Now that I am retired, when speaking to other retirees, I find that most of them have very few "personal friends" outside of their families. Most consider themselves lucky if they have two or three genuine friends—people who will stick with them regardless of their trials and tribulations. I consider myself very lucky to have a few really good friends—one of whom is my wife, Angel. I sincerely hope that each of you finds these friends during your lifetime.

Remember, each of us is an entrepreneur. Each of us is in charge of building our own life. Most of us cannot achieve our greatest potential without help from other professionals we meet along the way. We will need support from all of these "friends" during our lifetime, if we hope to achieve the "American Dream."

Choose Your Friends and Mentors

Wisely and Carefully

CHAPTER 22

Always Hire the
Best People

M any of us have heard the old adage: "First-rate people hire first-rate people, while second-rate people hire third-rate people." Experience has taught me that there is a lot of truth to this old adage.

I was hired as the new president to save three companies from financial failure. In each company, the owner had a management team that was second or third rate. They were averse to taking risks and were accustomed to agreeing with anything the owner said. They bowed to his every wish.

I was the opposite. When it came time to hire new members for my senior management teams, I applied the Golden Rule for hiring. I always hired "first-rate" candidates. I looked for a leader (not a follower)—someone who aspired to have my job as the Chief Operating Officer of the company. Why? Because if that new manager turned out to be as capable as he/she thought, then after they proved themselves through accomplishments, I was more than happy to reward them by turning over more of my daily responsibilities.

Why would I do such a stupid thing—encourage people to want my job? The answer is simple! If the highly capable people I hired could take over some or all of my day-to-day management responsibilities, then I would be free to spend more time on new technologies, acquisitions, and other activities that would grow our company.

I loved to help employees grow and become more successful in their jobs—because it made my job easier, and made our company more successful.

And, when assigning these managers more of my daily job responsibilities, I was happy to give them a promotion from Manager, to Vice President, to Senior Vice President or Executive Vice President—after they proved that they were deserving of an elevated title.

People are happy to be rewarded with new titles that represent and respect their contributions to an organization. For me, my title was irrelevant; the key was that our management team was making progress toward saving and rebuilding our struggling company. I always considered my title to be the "Head Janitor," because I was always cleaning up messes caused by other people. In the end, everybody won, and the company prospered.

I was very successful when applying this management philosophy to all of the failing companies that I saved from financial ruin, while rebuilding each into a national and/or international leader. And best of all, I never lost any of those highly capable and dedicated managers to other companies, even though our competitors tried to hire them away on many occasions. I thoroughly enjoyed the experience of building great leadership teams.

Oh, I did lose one manager. After she completed her PhD requirements, she left to become a vice-president of Indiana's finest vocational college. It was a pleasure to help her move on to her lifelong passion of education.

You see, good leaders never have a lack of growth opportunity for highly skilled and capable managers. Bad leaders are afraid to help their staff grow and move into positions of greater responsibility—primarily because of their own insecurities.

But, I must admit—it is rare to find a company that practices this Golden Rule when adding members to their management team. Why? Many managers are afraid to hire people who can challenge them or who could possibly step into their position. What a mistake these managers make! Their short-sightedness will hold their organizations back and prevent them from optimizing their growth and leadership in their respective industries. And, in reality, it will stunt or prevent the manager from achieving a higher degree of success in their own career.

Successful Leaders Hire Their Replacements

CHAPTER 23

Why Businesses Fail

" B ad Management" is the primary reason most organizations and businesses fail.

I have been challenged by a number of consultants regarding my opinion on this topic. In most cases, I have found that the arguments from business consultants were not valid—primarily because not one of those (so called) "experts" had ever been responsible for the hands-on management of a business turnaround! Experience has taught me that it is much easier to be a consultant than the person who actually walks into the fire to save a business from burning to the ground.

Having worked for an international CPA firm, I was exposed to the consulting business many years ago. Most consultants get hired to review business operations, identify problems, make recommendations on how to fix those problems, and determine what changes need to be made so the organization can become more efficient and profitable.

When doing so, most consultants have a treasure-trove of binders that are full of questionnaires and audit checklists. Next, the consultants interview company representatives and, in the end, regurgitate a management report that represents what company employees already knew, or should have known, if the company had good leadership on its senior management team.

In nearly every segment of American commerce, there are organizations and businesses that rank in the top 10% of their respective industry. Then there are those firms that make up 80% of their industry. Last are the bottom 10% that are struggling to survive—the stagnant and failing companies.

Of the failing companies for which I assumed the leadership position as president, each was failing because of bad management. This is the primary factor that separates highly successful companies from those firms that are failing or are in decline. I'm sure that others will argue with this statement, but the bottom line is that companies fail or excel based on the quality of their management team. Part III of this book will provide real-life proof to support my position on this topic. I turned failing companies into national and international leaders—and did so strictly through the use of "Good Leadership."

Having said this, there are significant benefits to being a consultant. There are also significant benefits for the current president of a failing company to hire a consultant, rather than hire a new senior manager to solve the problems that they created or allowed to develop during their management oversight.

For everyone involved, hiring an outside consultant is the safest decision. First, an outside consultant has a contract that guarantees payment when the consulting job is finished—and then the consultant goes away.

Second, it is less risky to be a consultant, because the consultant usually does not have any responsibility for implementing their recommendations within the failing organization and, therefore, will never be held accountable for producing results based on their recommendations!

Third, since most consultants report to the current president or owner of the company, all recommendations and draft reports are customarily reviewed with the president before a final report is issued. This practice gives the president, who probably is the real problem, an opportunity to "massage" the report so that no one on their management team will be embarrassed or offended by the consultant's observations.

Having personally experienced the foregoing practice, I have also seen consultants issue an "Executive Summary" that highlights the tougher problems—which are seen only by the president of the company. Many times these "Executive Summaries" are quickly filed away, to protect the managers who are causing the company's problems. After all, the president does not want to lose any members from his current management team—because he chose them.

From past experience, I can assure you that the current owner or president will not hold himself accountable for implementing the tough personnel changes that are needed to rebuild the company. But, at least they feel good for having hired an outside consulting expert who gave them some ideas. Then, after making a few minor changes, the management team will get back into the same old groove—until the company eventually fails or is sold.

However, when a new president is hired to rescue and rebuild a failing company, the owner is essentially admitting that he or she has failed to lead the company effectively. Therefore, the owner will expect quick results from the new president—because the company is already in the latter stages of market and/or financial failure! With a high degree of certainty, the new president (which I have been) is almost always walking into a hornets' nest and will surely experience a great deal of subversion from the management team that he or she will inherit. Why? Because these people are part of the bad management team that led the company into its current state of decline or failure!

After leaving public accounting, this small-town farm boy learned the hard way about the consequences of being hired as the new president of a failing company—that was owned by someone else. The expectation was that I would turn around and rebuild the company, but not make any changes that would ruffle management feathers in the process. *The "Birds of a Feather" would indeed "Flock Together."*

Complicating my turnaround job was the fact that I didn't realize that I had only three years to accomplish this difficult task.

During the first year, I had to identify the major problems and take corrective action. The second year, I had to show progress in the form of improved profits and financial stability. If this didn't happen, by the end of the third year, I was going to be fired. When heading up the turnaround of a failing company, there are no second chances, do-overs, or mulligans—as they would say in a friendly game of golf.

Now, you can consider the foregoing to be Bad News for the new president. But the fact is—there isn't any Good News. Bad News is bad, and Good News is bad—if the owner of the failing company remains involved after the new president arrives. Therefore, the new president can expect his/her employment to last only three years regardless of his/her level of success—and here is why.

During the first year, the new president must identify the major problems and take corrective action. The second year, the new leader must show progress in the form of improved profits and financial stability. And, if the company is progressing nicely, by the end of the third year, the new president will still get fired, because the owner who ran the company into the ground will reclaim his position as company president—because he is the owner and has the power to do so! More importantly, his ego and image as the leader need to be restored.

Yep, folks—Life Isn't Always Fair. I've been there and experienced everything I am sharing with you. This happened to me twice. But, having been taken advantage of by dishonest owners and having been pushed off of the proverbial turnip truck twice, I did not let this happen to this small-town farm boy again! Life is tough; we must learn from our experiences—and I (eventually) did.

One other important facet about failing businesses has to do with the rest of the management team who report to the owner. When the new leader (president) enters the scene, their top priority is to get rid of the new leader, before the new leader finds out that members of the existing management team are a major reason the business is failing. Their main goal is to stick together to protect their jobs and maintain the status quo. Bad managers find it very difficult to accept change and, therefore, unite to fight change.

This reaction is called the "Crab Mentality," studied by Dr. Tara Swart, a medical doctor, faculty at MIT Sloan, and award-winning author of "Neuroscience for Leadership." When crabs are trapped in a bucket and one of them attempts to climb out and escape, the others will pull the escaping crab back into the bucket. The group would rather all die together than let one crab escape. This mentality is very similar to the thoughts and actions of the existing management team in a failing company.

Dr. Swart stated that our human brains "are wired to avoid loss, twice as much as we are to get a reward." The fear of change that new leadership will bring into the company overrides their fear of the future, if changes are not made. Perhaps this helps explain why existing managers of a failing company don't jump at the opportunity to help the new president—and usually work against his efforts to implement changes that are necessary to successfully rebuild the failing business. In other words, they would rather all fail together than face the need for change. They are wired to "avoid loss" to their existing environment.

So, from the start, the new leader is probably doomed to a three-year tenure, and he/she will face an existing management team that is looking out for itself and not for the best interests of the company. I experienced this at each of the failing companies that I rescued and rebuilt.

What I also found interesting was the fact that, after firing the new president (me) who saved and rebuilt his company, and after the owner took back control of his company, the owner always kept the upgraded management team that I had hired and trained, because they were far better than the management team that the owner had in place when I arrived. And, the company owner always wants to keep the management team that helped implement the changes that saved and rebuilt his company. This always made him happy!

Having said this, the reader of this book should know that I was not a traditional business turnaround expert. Most "turnaround experts" employ very different strategies than I used. The first actions taken by many "turnaround experts" are to lay off personnel, drastically cut costs in areas such as product development, and reduce advertising expenses, etc. I took none of those actions. *I never laid off a single employee during my entire career*—and I fired only one person.

Instead, as president, I eliminated management corruption, operating inefficiencies, and waste—while rebuilding and expanding the business through the use of new technology and entering international markets. You see, failed management is nearly always the problem—not the workers. *I never punished workers for failures that were caused by their bosses.* To do so would have been very unfair, because it was management who got the bigger paychecks, and it was the management team who caused the company to be in a state of decline or failure.

As a hands-on president, for each failing company, I first studied the internal financial statements, to identify areas of the operations for which I had a concern. Then, I went into each department and reviewed their procedures, while participating directly in the daily operations—whether it was in sales, customer service, purchasing, or production.

After asking a few questions, the problems became clear—not just to me, but also to the manager who was in charge of that department. And, guess what? Nearly every time, those managers found another job and left the company. I then trained someone else to gradually take over the former manager's daily responsibilities, while I expanded my involvement into other problem areas of the company.

As mentioned earlier, I had to fire only one person during my entire career, because when the underperforming managers understood that I knew that they were the problem—the rats jumped off the ship and swam to shore! Many took employment with competitors, which was good for my company.

Next, rather than cutting back on product development, I focused on improving our products by integrating new technologies into the business and broadening the company's sales, both domestically and into international markets.

My experiences have proven to me that having a management team that promotes change, and being a leader in technology, is a winning combination that will assure the growth and profitability of most businesses.

The fact that Bad Management is the primary cause of business failures will be discussed extensively in Part III, where I review six companies, from different industries, in which I experienced the consequences of bad management.

Bad Management Causes Business Failures

CHAPTER 2 4

Is the American Dream Just a Dream?

I s the "American Dream Real"? Can it still be achieved today—or is it just a dream?

Let me assure you—"The American Dream Is Real," and it is out there, waiting for you. But, *you have to want it*—and *you will have to earn it. It is not free!*

During my career, I came to realize that people have many reasons for failing to achieve the "American Dream," some of which were discussed in previous chapters. I believe there are a few other major reasons for their lack of success.

First, I found that many people fail to achieve the "American Dream" because of their ego. These people continue to believe that *"Life is All About Them."*

During my career of turning around and rebuilding failing companies, I also observed that every one of those companies was managed by a chief executive officer who thought they were *"The Smartest Person in the Room"* and that they knew all the answers. Yet, their company was failing! ***This is a character flaw that every young adult should understand and strive to avoid.***

There is an old adage from Lord Acton, a British historian, that states: "Power Corrupts, and Absolute Power Corrupts Absolutely." There is a lot of truth to this adage—in government and in the business world. Too many people have their careers cut short or fail to achieve their full potential because they become full of themselves and believe that they are smarter than everyone else as they climbed the ladder of success in their career—and then they become dictators, instead of leaders. So, some of the leadership problems that caused the failure of Socialist governments in the countries of Cuba, Zimbabwe, and Venezuela can also be found in the leadership of failing organizations right here in the USA.

There is another adage that states: "God gave us two eyes, two ears, and one mouth." I believe there is a good reason for this, and that is—we learn by listening and seeing; however, we learn very little when we are talking.

Those who think that they are the smartest people in the room usually talk too much and observe and listen too little—thus losing out on important learning opportunities. Their next step is usually to become a ruthless dictator. As Lord Acton said: "Power Corrupts, and Absolute Power Corrupts Absolutely."

I guess you could say that I was lucky, because I grew up with low self-esteem and a deflated ego. During my childhood and adolescence, my dad and my high school counselor made sure that I understood that I was nothing but a small-town farm boy who would never achieve any degree of success in life. I was told not to go to college, because I couldn't succeed. I clearly understood that I was not the "Smartest Person in the Room."

Looking back over my life, I guess that being raised under those conditions on a farm in Indiana might have been a very good thing, because a big ego never became an impediment during my pursuit of the "American Dream."

Another major reason people fail to achieve the American Dream is because they fail to establish a Personal Strategic Plan that will lead to success. As the old adage states: *"If you don't know where you are headed, any ole road will get you there."* These are also the people who "let life happen to them," rather than take control over the 80–90% of their lives that they can control.

Unfortunately, by the time most people reach their late 20s, they have already established a lifestyle pattern that is difficult to change. That is why I tell today's youth that the decisions they make during the next 5–10 years will have a profound effect on their future lifestyle and economic security.

What is your Personal Strategic Plan? Remember, you are the CEO and are in charge of your own company. *You are the leader—so plan accordingly.*

Many people also fail to achieve the "American Dream" because they become more inflexible as they age. Folks, we are living in a world that is changing at the fastest pace that humans have ever experienced. We must embrace change to its fullest, throughout our lives—or we will be left behind.

In fact, we should look for ways to make our companies and our careers obsolete—before somebody else does it to us! Let me use the following business-turnaround situation as an example.

Most of my competitors in the printing industry laughed at me when I took control of an insolvent company that was more than $2.5 million in debt and couldn't make its payroll. After all, I had zero experience in the printing industry, while most of my competitors were multi-generational family businesses or were run by people who had been in the printing industry for decades. This attitude was not a surprise to me, because I had experienced this same lack of respect from competitors in other industries, when I rebuilt other failing companies. Guess what? They aren't laughing anymore!

One of the first things I did as president of the failing printing company was to quickly understand the technology and capabilities of my competitors and the broader national network of support that existed. From this, I learned that "printers printed, and finishers did the finishing." There were no exceptions to this unwritten rule in our markets.

Well, I have never supported "unwritten rules" among industry competitors. Therefore, my wife, Angel, and I promised a major US publisher that, with a purchasing commitment from them, our company would quickly move to become a one-stop supply source and the only company in the Midwest that could do all of the printing and specialty finishing in-house for high-end, fancy book covers in their computer and education markets.

By becoming a one-stop supply source, we would be able to provide incredible benefits to this major publisher because we would be able to gain total control over product quality, while greatly improving delivery times, and reducing the price they were paying for high-quality book covers. Wow, what a risk we took—but a risk that helped pull us out of insolvency and turn our firm into a viable growth company.

Our competitors hated us, because they didn't want to see change come into the industry. They were happy with the status quo.

My wife and I constantly evaluated how we could pursue new technologies and processes. We searched for ways to obsolesce our current business operations, before our competitors had a chance to catch up with us. When doing so, we established technology partnerships with major international suppliers, which helped propel our firm into a national leadership position.

Our competitors stopped laughing at us along the way. In fact, about 75% of our original competitors, including our largest local competitor, went out of business during the 15 years that my wife and I spent rebuilding our company.

Yes, this is the Digital Age—and here we were, competing in the industry of printed material! Yet, through innovation and new technology, our company grew by more than 600% and became a national leader. Our technology and quality were so good that we even exported our printed material to other countries—boy, that's a switch from what we read about in today's news!

The lesson to be learned from this is that, with whatever career we pursue, we should always embrace change and consider it to be our best friend. In fact, we should search for ways to regularly incorporate change into our lives, because, in reality, *changes are windows of opportunity.* Change can be exciting and fun!

Another major reason people fail to achieve the "American Dream" is that when the going gets tough, they quit and settle back into a less-threatening existence. Everyone stumbles and falls. But, we must get back on track with our Personal Strategic Plan, if we expect to fully experience the "American Dream."

As Dr. Phil likes to say: "Get Real." Life is not a fairytale, and the "American Dream" is not something just to be dreamed. It must be earned. Otherwise, everyone would be living the "American Dream," and none of us would have any appreciation or derive any real joy from the achievements we make in life.

As this ole farm boy would say: "If dreams were reality, then pigs would fly." Not surprisingly, we never raised a pig on our farm that could fly, and we didn't have any neighbors who raised pigs that could fly. Maybe that's why I quit dreaming and chose to work my butt off to achieve the "American Dream."

I know that I have said this before—but I'm going to say it again. You and I are privileged to be citizens of this wonderful country we call the United States of America, which operates under the principles of a "Free-Enterprise System."

Now that I am retired, I look back at my travels throughout the world. When doing so, I think of the billions of people who are born in countries where they have little or no opportunity to achieve the level of success that is available to us in America.

Then, I ask myself: *"Why did our Creator choose to bless us with the privilege of being born in the United States of America? Why were we given this privilege?"* Why wasn't this privilege given to someone else, such as to a child born into a poverty-stricken country, where that child will never have an opportunity to achieve the "American Dream"? *I don't have answers to these questions. Do you?*

I will be forever grateful to my Creator for the opportunities that were available to me in our country, *America—the Land of Incredible Freedom and Opportunity—for all of its citizens!*

The American Dream Is Real

So

Go Out and Earn It!

CHAPTER 25

Who Wants to Follow in My Footsteps?

A few years back, I was speaking at a women's conference in Indianapolis. Following my talk, a young woman approached me and stated that she had just received her MBA from Harvard and, after hearing my talk, she thought it would be a great experience to get into the business of turning around failing companies. The following is some of the conversation we shared.

First, following in my footsteps is easy. Otherwise this small-town, naive farm boy probably wouldn't have found so many opportunities along this career path.

There are thousands of failing or poorly performing companies all over the United States. They run the gamut of businesses, from manufacturing, to distribution, to wholesale, to retail, to banking, etc. Some are local, while others are regional, national, or international in market coverage.

In any event, there are plenty of opportunities to enter these companies in a senior management position, if you have a good education, a reasonable degree of professional background, and a proven track record of success. The owners and/or presidents of many of these failing businesses are eager for someone else to take over the challenge of saving and/or rebuilding the company that they ran into the ground. *I was their life jacket—and was hired to save them from drowning.*

People have asked me, "Why are there so many of these opportunities?" The answer is simple. Most companies fail because of Bad Management—starting at the top. There are many bad managers out there. Just look at all of the underperforming or failing businesses!

This is especially true in businesses that are managed by 2nd- or 3rd-generation family owners. These owners typically have not had to experience the struggle or make the sacrifices that were necessary for their parents or grandparents to start and build their successful businesses.

These folks are rarely entrepreneurs and have an aversion to risk-taking. Statistically, the majority of family-owned businesses fail during the 2nd generation. By the end of the 3rd generation, very few, if any, are still family owned. They either fail or are sold.

Let's face it, if the current business owner and his/her management team had the ability to save or rebuild their company, they would have already done so. Therefore, it is clear that they do not have the leadership on their management team that is capable of taking on this difficult challenge.

But wait—I have found that this is not always the case! In fact, other members of the existing management team might have the ability to lead such an effort, but they don't want to take on the responsibility of doing so. Why? The answer pertains to "self-preservation."

Other management personnel don't want to risk their current position or their future by taking on a risky challenge, which very likely would end up making the owner or other members of the management team look bad.

Or, this existing management person might not succeed with his/her attempt to turn around the failing company.

Either way, an existing manager could very well end up losing his/her comfortable job during the turnaround process. At a minimum, they would upset the status quo and would lose the trust of the other "good ole boys and good ole gals" with whom they work.

However, if someone (such as me) is hired from the outside to turn around a failing company, there are other consequences that will materialize—as you will read in Part III of this book.

Therefore, being hired as president to salvage a failing company while assuming leadership responsibility over the existing management team is very risky for an outsider—especially if that person does not have the right to end up as the majority owner of the company, if and when they succeed with the business turnaround.

Remember, the current management team has only one goal, and that is to preserve their positions in the company. They don't want to change. They want the new president to go away. To them, self-preservation comes first!

Therefore, recognizing the high level of risk that the new president of a turnaround company will be assuming, he/she should have a written contract that guarantees that they will receive quantifiable performance bonuses, based on achievement of specific, measurable financial goals—or that they will have an absolute right to purchase the company at a pre-determined price, should they succeed in saving the company from financial ruin.

If a purchase arrangement is not possible, then the new president should insist on a financial payout, should he/she be terminated. Without this safety net, the incoming president will be taking all of the risks, with no "cushion," should they get fired after they have done all of the hard work of saving and rebuilding the failing company.

If contractual arrangements are not assured (up front), then the incoming president will (in all probability) face termination—whether they succeed or fail with the business turnaround. As you will read in Part III of this book, I have been there and experienced this fact, twice in my career—each time after I succeeded in saving and rebuilding the failing company. I finally learned my lesson, got smarter, and didn't let it happen a third time!

In conclusion, following in my footsteps is easier than one might think, because there are many failing or poorly performing companies around. But, taking on the responsibility for turning around and rebuilding these companies is fraught with personal and professional risks, and in many instances, there will not be a safety net to protect the incoming president after the turnaround has been completed.

And so, I told this young lady that it really is quite easy to find opportunities to follow in my footsteps. This is exactly how I learned the different definitions of "friends," what it is like to become the stale bagel that is left over from yesterday's breakfast buffet, and how it feels to be pushed off the proverbial turnip truck or hay wagon after all of the hard work has been completed.

Would I recommend this type of career to others? Maybe, but my type of career is certainly not for everyone. However, it provides an example of our real world and the struggles, backstabbing, and other challenges that most of us will face (to one degree or another) while trying to build our future.

After hearing of my struggles, and the betrayals that I experienced—

She Chose a Different Career

CHAPTER 2 6

Life Is Short

As stated at the beginning, life is short, very short. Yet, each of us has this life, in which we have a golden opportunity to live the "American Dream."

I acknowledge that living the "American Dream" does not have the same meaning for everyone.

However, for most of us, living the "American Dream" includes the desire to make a meaningful contribution to society by being self-sufficient, having a challenging and rewarding career, raising our families, having financial stability during our career and throughout our retirement years, and being respected as we leave this Earth and return to our spiritual world.

In Part III of this book, "My Life as an Entrepreneur—A Road Less Traveled," you will read about the struggles and challenges that I faced when building my career as a CPA and International Entrepreneur. This segment covers many of the betrayals I experienced along the way—from colleagues and from business owners.

You will also learn about the company that my wife, Angel, and I purchased and saved from bankruptcy. I hope my experiences will motivate all young men and women to begin drafting and then completing their Personal Strategic Plan.

And, please remember: **Success does not come easy. We must earn it!** As I said earlier—"If dreams were reality, then the pigs we raised on our farm would fly."

At the end of this life, each of us should be proud of ourselves if we have achieved two goals. First, let's hope that our souls have grown and matured in a positive way, from our many experiences in this life. Remember, we can learn something positive from most of our experiences.

Second, let's hope that we have helped many other people (and puppies) along the way—and practiced good morals, values, and ethics, as we leave this world to those who follow us.

Have a wonderful life—while pursuing your "American Dream."

Life Is Short

Make the Most of It

PART III

My Life as an Entrepreneur
A Road Less Traveled

From a Small-Town Farm Boy, to a
CPA and International Entrepreneur

Background

*T**he "American Dream Is Real."* Today's youth can accomplish nearly anything they seek to achieve in life—*if they are willing to pay the price.*

The main reason for providing background on "My Life as an Entrepreneur" is to reach out to those students and young adults who believe they have little or no hope of achieving the "American Dream."

After reading this book, I hope that everyone realizes that if this small-town farm boy could achieve a level of success that was way beyond anything he could have imagined, then they, too, can achieve the "American Dream."

Second, I want the readers of this book to realize that I experienced the many realities of life that were detailed in Part I and Part II of this book, and did so after being raised with good morals, values, and ethics that seem to be (sadly) slipping away from many people in today's society.

Then again, after reading Part III, you might wonder if good morals, values, and ethics ever really existed in our society, because most of the betrayals I experienced came from older people, many of whom preached the benefits of good morals, values, and ethics in church every Sunday. So, maybe I was the odd one—a square peg trying to fit into a round world? You can be the judge.

Throughout my life I have championed higher education and opportunities for women and minorities. During my career I hired and promoted more women into management positions than men.

At Ball State University, while working my way through college, as the manager and caretaker of the College-Main Apartments, I converted the apartment complex into married-student housing and recruited the first minority couples to live in our building. Those couples were wonderful members of our community, and we had great times together.

As I look back on my career, I am humbled by the many professional women and minorities with whom I had the opportunity to share this experience that we call "life." I would not have become the person or success that I am without their help. I thank each and every one of them for their kindness and friendship.

Life Is a Journey—
Let's Enjoy Our Time Together

CHAPTER 28

In the Beginning

I was raised on a run-down farm near a small town called Hoagland, in northeast Indiana. Our dad made all three of us boys help clear and burn the trees from our property so we could farm the land. This started at the age of five years old, and to this day, I clearly remember the bitterly cold winters my brothers and I spent clearing that land. The only good lesson we learned from this experience was that if we worked hard enough, even in cold weather, we would not freeze.

Our dad did not like people who had an education beyond high school—probably because that is where his education had stopped. And, if a high school education was good enough for him, it was good enough for everyone else, because he was certain that he was the smartest guy around. Unfortunately, this attitude also made him feel superior to women—whom he belittled and demeaned. *It was from him that I learned how "not to treat women."*

Our mother was raised by a single parent after her father died from the flu when she was a small child. Her mother reminded me of Lily Tomlin, who played "Ernestine" on the TV show *Laugh-In*.

Both were switchboard operators for the telephone company and sat at a switchboard day after day, putting in and pulling out telephone wires to connect callers to one another.

This was the first self-sufficient woman I ever met in my life. My grandmother worked her entire life and never relied on anyone, or on our government, to provide her with financial support while raising her daughter—and what a wonderful job she did in raising her daughter, who then became a wonderful mother to us. *May God bless her soul, as she and my mother soar with God's angels.*

Despite her few opportunities as a child, our mother graduated as valedictorian of her high school class in Van Wert, Ohio, and then worked her way through medical training to become a Registered Nurse. She was a very gentle and loving soul who encouraged her children to excel, despite our dad's negativism.

My grandmother and my mother were the first Heroes in my life.

Mothers Are Very Special

I lost my mother way too soon

CHAPTER 29

High School

Our dad demanded that we work on the farm before doing any studying. I was an academic underachiever in high school—a significant underachiever.

From the start, I was bullied by the junior and senior athletes, who would push and abuse me as I walked down the hallways between classes. They weren't happy about the fact that the high school coach had chosen this "outsider" to start on the junior varsity basketball team.

In my sophomore year, the basketball team was to assemble at the high school gym and travel in assigned cars to scout a rival team that was playing about 30 miles away. Since I was not old enough to drive, I was assigned to ride with an older teammate— who left me standing in the parking lot, while he drove off with other players, whose families were related to each other.

During my entire high school experience, I was never invited to anyone's birthday party, nor was I ever part of any close-knit group of kids in my class. After all, I was an "outsider," because my family wasn't born in that small farming community—and I wasn't related to any of the other students.

Following graduation, many of those students remained in the Hoagland area and still cling to their little cliques. And sadly, some of those who left and had a career outside of Hoagland found that when they did return—they were no longer welcomed back into the "flock" that they left following graduation. Remember the old adage that "Birds of a Feather Flock Together." Most people will discover that this old adage is very true—both in their personal lives and in their careers.

The foregoing situation reminds me of another scientific finding called the "Crab Mentality," which was discussed in Part II, **"Why Businesses Fail."** Again, you will find that the "Crab Mentality" is a mindset that we will experience in our personal and professional lives. This is sad—because we can learn so much from "outsiders" and people with backgrounds that are different from ours, versus the birds of a feather who flock together, in little cliques.

As you can see, bullying was just as prevalent during the 1960s, or maybe more so, than it is today. During my teenage years, nobody in the school system thought anything about it—nor did they do anything about it. So, it really doesn't matter whether a teenager is raised in a small farming community or in a big city—bullying exists, and people can be mean to each other! But, that's life, folks. We have to take the bad with the good, get tougher with ourselves—and move forward in a positive direction with our lives. Otherwise, we let the bullies win!

During our senior year, my high school counselor, Mr. Justice, said: "Evan, don't go to college, because you won't make it." Wow, what a wonderful confidence builder! You see—I was one of those students who helped make the upper half of our class the academic leaders. In fact, that was probably my greatest accomplishment in my graduating class of about 39 students!

Other than my mother, I did have one additional supporter, and that was the high school basketball coach, Mark Schoeff, who said, "Evan, after graduation, get as far away from Hoagland as you can, because there is a great big world out there for you to experience."

After graduation, I took Coach Schoeff's advice, left Hoagland, Indiana, and never looked back at the small town where I had been raised. How fortunate I was to have a mother and a coach in my life, who saw a future for me—that extended beyond our small farming community!

Since I believed in my mother and I trusted Coach Schoeff, I left my past behind—except for my memories. In doing so, I left with a huge amount of anger toward my dad and Mr. Justice, neither of whom had any confidence in me. This kind of anger will either break a person's spirit or make them very angry—to the point that they want to prove the naysayers wrong.

This is when I took control of my life—and I thank my Creator for giving me a fighting spirit that I didn't know was in me, until I had to make a choice to: Give up on life and prove the naysayers right or leave the only life I had ever known, and attempt to prove the naysayers wrong.

In retrospect, I now realize that both my mother and Coach Schoeff developed this fighting spirit within me. My mother overcame an impoverished childhood, and became a Registered Nurse. My high school coach constantly challenged me by putting me into difficult situations. As a sophomore, the coach challenged me to become the center on our high school varsity basketball team—which I did by out-rebounding and out-shooting a senior who was six inches taller than me. Still, it wasn't until many years later that I began to fully appreciate the advice from my coach, who told me to get as far away from Hoagland as I could, because there was a great big world out there for me to experience.

Later, I was very fortunate to have called Coach Schoeff just weeks before his unexpected passing, to thank him for his guidance and encouragement.

Goodbye, Hoagland
Hello, World

CHAPTER 30

Vocational School

After leaving the farm, my first job was peeling potatoes at McDonald's. Yes, as stated earlier, years ago they really did peel potatoes to make the French fries at McDonald's. After leaving work at McDonald's, I went to a second job, where I worked as a grease-monkey, servicing cars at a Firestone Store in Fort Wayne, Indiana.

At both of these jobs I was paid $0.80 *per hour.* On the farm, dad paid us $0.50 *per week*—if he had the money. *Wow, I thought I was getting rich!*

After doing this work for about six months (which was easier than farm work), I saved enough money to enroll at International Business College, a two-year vocational school. To many folks, that was a strange thing for me to do, since I had never had a business course in high school, and there was nothing in my family history to suggest that this might be an education I should pursue.

The real reason I chose this school was because I was determined to further my education beyond high school and, in those days, International Business College was the only vocational school around. So, I had no other choice.

At International Business College, for the first time, I found a group of very intelligent people (nerds) who included me in their group. Wow, did this change my life! Although I had never taken a business course before, I was determined to study hard, stay in school, and keep my nerdy friends. As with many student-friends, upon graduation, we immediately lost track of each other—forever.

To this day, I have no idea about how good my Grade Point Average was; however, it must have been quite good, because upon graduation with my two-year Associate's Degree in Accounting, I was the only graduate from International Business College to be hired to work at the corporate headquarters of Marathon Oil Company, in Findlay, Ohio.

Wow! For this small-town Indiana farm boy, moving to Ohio seemed like traveling to a foreign country—and now I was going to be working at a Fortune 500 Company!

From McDonald's
to Marathon Oil Company

CHAPTER 31

Marathon Oil Company

Joining Marathon Oil Company was a life-changing experience. There, I was the only newly hired two-year graduate working with four-year college graduates from all over the United States. Until then, I had lived in a small-town farming community for my entire life. So, I went from being a Hoosier (whatever that is) to being a Buckeye (a nut from a tree). *A "nut"—that sounds about right!* ☺

During my time at Marathon, I was surprised to learn that my financial education at the vocational school allowed me to compete effectively with the four-year college graduates who sat next to me in the various departments in which I worked.

Then, I was selected to play on Marathon's traveling fast-pitch softball team. We played at other colleges and at federal prisons. Wow, what an experience for a 19-year old kid from Hoagland, Indiana, especially since I wasn't legally old enough to play sports against inmates in a federal prison—but, I did!

I will never forget my first base hit at a federal prison. While standing on first base, the inmate told me that he was in jail for attempted murder. Holy Cow—the hair stood up on the back of my neck! I had never met a person who tried to kill another human. In my youth, I never even shot at rabbits or pheasants when my family went hunting on the farm.

Then, two years later, Frank McClain, a vice president of Marathon Oil Company, pulled me aside and very nicely told me to go back to college and get a four-year degree. He stated that he saw great potential in me but couldn't really help my career unless I had a four-year college degree.

Wow! Was he kicking me out of Marathon, or was he really trying to help me? Either way, I was being told that my career with Marathon would be limited. So, I quickly realized how important it was to have a four-year college degree—if I was to continue working for this company.

Thank you, Frank McClain, for your advice and for giving me the gentle nudge that I needed to return for my four-year degree. As I learned several years later, you were truly doing me a favor—when you asked me to return to Marathon.

Life Is a Marathon—Not a Sprint

Ball State University

With a car and only $1,000 in the bank, I enrolled at Ball State University in Muncie, Indiana. I was lucky, because in those days, the state-supported universities had to accept all Indiana high school graduates. What I didn't know was that the University was going to enroll me on academic probation, because my admission scores were very low.

My counselor wanted me to spend my first year taking "remedial" courses, before mainstreaming into the normal class schedule. I told her that I did not have the financial ability to take "remedial" courses. So, Ball State started my classes during summer school, probably thinking that I would flunk out before the "real students" showed up in September.

To make matters tougher, I had to work two jobs to pay for my tuition, books, and living expenses—and I was in the Army Reserves. You see, I didn't qualify for academic scholarships or grants for needy students. I qualified for nothing—except academic probation! Things weren't getting easier!

As I said before, this kind of adversity can either make or break a person. Inside my heart, I knew I could get the job done and graduate from Ball State, because I had competed very effectively with four-year graduates from all over the United States when I worked at Marathon Oil Company. *So, it was at this time that I decided that, if everyone attending Ball State was smarter than me, then I was going to outwork them.* Because, one great value I got from my dad was that I learned how to work hard—very hard!

At the end of my first year at Ball State, I received a letter from Victor B. Lawhead, the Dean of Undergraduate Programs (I still have his letter) asking me to join the Honors Program, because I had one of the top GPAs at Ball State. I informed him that I could not join the Honors Program, because I was on academic probation.

Well, you guessed it—one hour later I was no longer on academic probation. Wow! My head was spinning. My hard work was paying off.

While at Ball State, I had two professors ask me not to take their final exam, because my high test scores were preventing them from awarding an "A" to any of the other students in my class. This was hard to fathom for a small-town farm boy who graduated in the bottom half of his high school class.

In another class, following our first test, the instructor told me that he would give me an "A" for the course—*if I promised not to show up for any more classes*. However, if I insisted on continuing with his course, there were going to be problems, because I was academically too advanced for the level of teaching in his class. Being the obedient young man that I was, I didn't show up for any more of his classes—and sure enough, he awarded me an "A" for the course! ☺

During my junior year, my mother died from a brain tumor. Like many other people, I never got over the loss of my mother.

She was kind and supportive of everything I tried to accomplish in life. I'm sorry she did not get to attend my graduation. She would have been so happy. *I love you mom, and miss you very much.*

While at Ball State, I was the only student from outside the Political Science Department to win a seat on the Model United Nations program in New York City. I was allowed to enter this contest because I was taking my one and only Political Science class at that time. I did a significant amount of research and won a competitive speech contest to secure my place on the team.

Boy, did the Political Science majors hate that! Their college program was being infiltrated by a student from the College of Business—which was not supposed to happen!

This turned out to be a terrific experience for me, because I had never traveled beyond Ohio, and certainly had never visited New York City—where I saw my first street mugging. Wow, that was a real shock for this small-town farm boy!

As mentioned earlier, while at Ball State, I worked several jobs—including managing and maintaining a seventeen-unit apartment complex, called the "College-Main Apartments," located behind the Student Center. While at Ball State, I was able to convert the apartments into married-student housing, and recruited the first minority students into the apartment complex. We had great times together. This helped set the stage for the remainder of my life, when I worked with and then hired many minorities—and loved every minute when doing so. I thank my Creator that he/she raised this small-town farm boy in an environment that fostered acceptance of every American citizen.

During the last month of my senior year, I was shocked when the Dean of the College of Business informed me that I had been assigned to sit in the front row at graduation, with Honor Graduates from the other colleges. Prior to this, I had never been informed that I was among the top students at Ball State—except when the Dean of Students removed me from the list of those who were on "academic probation," after my first year at Ball State.

At graduation, I didn't even receive congratulations from my dad for getting my degree or for graduating with honors—or for working and paying my way through college. Boy, talk about getting kicked in the stomach and being brought back to the reality of the world in which I was raised! But, my mother's spirit was there, and I know she was very proud of me. ***Thanks, Mom!***

But remember, my dad did teach me how to work. So, I never let anyone outwork me during my life, with one exception—and that is my wife, Angel, who works rings around me and loves every minute of it. Again, following our graduation ceremony, I never again saw or had contact with any of my fellow classmates. These "friends" pursued different careers and met new "friends" in their lives.

While at Ball State, I worked full-time and paid for all of my education. I graduated with no debt. But, I will tell you, it would have been nice to have received some kind of financial assistance, so that I could have enjoyed a bit more of the college experience. Instead, it was work, work, work—just like my days back on the farm. However, this might have been a blessing in disguise because, as it turned out, my experiences on the farm and at Ball State University strengthened my resolve to face the challenges that were about to confront me in my professional career.

During my last term at Ball State, I didn't even have a chance to sign up for job interviews. Numerous companies contacted me at my home, including my former employer, Marathon Oil Company.

Choosing my first job out of college was a tough decision, because Frank McClain, the vice president of Marathon, who encouraged me to return to college, badly wanted me to return to Marathon and work with his international audit staff. I did not return to Marathon because I didn't want to become a "little spoke in a great big wheel"—one among thousands of employees.

Instead, *I wanted to pursue a career that would challenge my education and push me to excel at an even higher level.*

Upon reflection, it was at Ball State that I found that I was never satisfied with the results that I produced—probably because I started out on academic probation, and few people other than my mother, my high school basketball coach, and Frank McClain had any confidence in my ability to succeed. So, I ignored yesterday's accomplishments and pushed myself every day to do better. As a result, there were many academic quarters for which I received a 4.0 (A) average.

Over the years, I have asked myself why I had this determination to succeed. Every time, I reached the same conclusion. I kept pushing myself to prove to my dad and my high school counselor that they were wrong. I was determined to become more than just a small-town farm boy from Hoagland, Indiana, who graduated in the lower half of his class of approximately 39 students.

As I stated earlier, *anger, when channeled in a positive direction, can produce positive results,* including achievement of the "American Dream."

Life is a journey; it is not a sprint. So, I kept running toward the future!

Later in this book, you will read that Ball State started a major (now a minor) in International Business, as a result of my career.

What an Experience!

Thank You, Ball State University

First Job After College

Instead of returning to Marathon Oil Company, I accepted a position with an international CPA firm that was one of the largest audit, tax, and advisory firms of the 1970s, and still is today.

This position allowed me to apply my college education to the real world of manufacturing, insurance, banking, wholesale distribution, government audits, financial reporting, taxation, and management consulting. In addition, with this international CPA firm, I received extensive summer training that helped raise my education and career to a level that I could not have experienced anywhere else. During this time, I became a CPA and studied business law in the MBA program at Indiana University. This course proved to be invaluable during my career, because every business has legal issues that must be addressed.

Please remember, *the first job a person takes after college is possibly the most important career decision they will make during their entire life,* because it establishes the base from which our careers will either grow or stagnate.

Then, after working for several years with exceptionally talented professionals and thinking that my career was really progressing, my world collapsed and came tumbling down. My firm announced a major staff layoff, because their audit contract with the federal government had run out of funding.

Wow, my career went from the top to the bottom—and there I was, looking up and wondering, *"What just happened?"* I felt like someone had kicked me into a street gutter—face down! But, I refused to let this setback control my life. *I refused to quit on myself—and you should never quit on yourself!* During my career with this CPA firm, I had the opportunity to audit many companies, some of which were managed very poorly.

With this knowledge, I believed that I could do a pretty good job in a management position with a manufacturing company.

Choose Your First Job Carefully

It Will Affect the Rest of Your Career

CHAPTER 34

First Management
Position

S o, having earned my CPA License, I got back on my feet and
searched for a management position in a manufacturing company.
I ended up with a medical-device company that was struggling
financially and having a difficult time.

I was hired to become the company's next Chief Financial
Officer; however, my initial duties related to corporate development, which meant that I took over the company's legal problems,
its information systems, and other problem areas that no one else
wanted to handle. This is the first place where my graduate law
course became a real asset during my career.

In essence, I was jumping into a frying pan, and didn't realize
the complicated professional life that I was about to enter. But,
I loved taking on challenges and tackling problems. *I actually
thought that this was going to be fun!*

Although I learned a lot about corporate litigation, design
engineering, manufacturing, and quality control, it became clear

that the owner of the company was a major impediment and was holding back the growth potential of his own company.

My major achievement in this position was that I did save the company from bankruptcy by settling a lawsuit that was caused by the runaway egos of the owner and a senior manager of the firm. I ended up settling the lawsuit without paying a dime, by reinstating the employee who had filed the litigation, claiming that he had been wrongfully terminated—which was true!

This employee was the company's top sales performer and had been improperly fired from his employment contract—solely because his ego clashed with that of his boss, the vice president of sales. So, losing this litigation would have been ruinous to the company.

But, boy did I take a lot of heat from both sides while trying to develop a solution that would work for everybody. In the end, settling this lawsuit was truly in the best interest of everyone.

You Can't Please Everyone, Every Time

A Lesson from the School of Hard Knocks

CHAPTER 35

From the Frying Pan—
Into the Fire, and
Purdue University

It was then that I was recruited to become the Corporate Controller of a public company that was the third largest electric meter and electronics manufacturer in the United States, located in Lafayette, Indiana—near Purdue University, where I spent a great deal of time with engineering professors, who were my neighbors. To this date, Angel and I maintain strong contacts with Purdue, which is the home of one of the world's finest Veterinary Colleges that is a world-leader in cancer research. More about Purdue a bit later.

Now, back to my new position. I soon learned from the VP of Finance that the company had been experiencing multi-million-dollar inventory shrinkages for a number of years and that the five Corporate Controllers (all CPAs) who preceded me had not solved the problem—and all got fired.

I was then informed that if I didn't solve the problem during my first year with the company, the V P of Finance was going get fired; however, before he got fired, he was going to fire me. Wow, I truly did go from a frying pan into a fire!

I spent the next four months at the company's Dayton, Ohio subsidiary that manufactured electronic equipment. This facility accounted for more than $1 million of the company's annual inventory shortage.

The General Manager of this facility hated to see me. After all, I was the sixth Corporate Controller in recent years, and none of the others had solved the massive inventory-shortage problem. On my first day at his plant, the General Manager introduced me to his staff as *"the s.o.b. from the home office, who has all of the answers."* Wow, I was off to a great start!

I spent days and nights observing the plant's operations and soon realized that accounting department personnel stayed in their office and had no interaction with the plant, unless someone from the plant visited their office. Otherwise, it was just paper transfers between the two departments. I saw them as paper-shuffling Bean Counters. They were not financial managers.

I spent many nights on the manufacturing floor. There, I noticed that large, 55-gallon drums were staged throughout the plant. Upon inspection, I found that faulty electronic components were thrown into those barrels and sent to the local dump for disposal, with no reporting of this scrap to the accounting department. So, it was no wonder that this plant was experiencing a huge inventory shortage every year. Expensive electronic components and wiring harnesses were being sent to the local dump every week—with no financial reporting.

After emptying several of the drums, inspecting each piece, and calculating the value of waste in each drum, I estimated the value of this unreported waste on an annual basis.

Then, I took a big risk and asked for the plant to be shut down at the end of six months, so that an inventory could be taken. Based on the plant's level of manufacturing activity, I expected to find a $500,000 inventory shortage. Well, I was close, very close. The actual shortage was $502,000. Wow! Not bad for a farm boy from the small town of Hoagland, Indiana—who nearly flunked high school math! See, *if I can accomplish this, then so can you!*

I then found that this flawed manufacturing process was also the cause of the inventory shortage at the company's Lafayette, Indiana plant. Finding the cause for the company's year-end inventory shortages, and saving the company from giving another embarrassing explanation to the Securities and Exchange Commission and to its shareholders made all the difference in the world for my career.

I was immediately promoted to Chief Financial Officer, reporting directly to the president of the company, where I became his right-hand advisor. I was also put in charge of overseeing the company's six other operating divisions throughout the United States.

However, I insisted that the company retain its VP of Finance and let him handle the treasury functions, until he qualified for retirement. This might sound stupid to many readers, but—I was not about to walk over someone else to get ahead in my career, especially since this person was nearing sixty years of age (those were my values).

This turned out to be an extensive place of employment in my life, during which I spent many hours with scientists at our company and with professors at Purdue University.

Later, my firm went through lengthy takeover negotiations—one with US Industries (a huge US conglomerate) and the other with Landis & Gyr, from Switzerland. We ended up with Landis & Gyr. I was one of only two corporate officers who were retained after the merger. Everyone else was immediately replaced by a management team from Landis & Gyr.

My time with Landis & Gyr was very enlightening. I learned how the Europeans conducted their worldwide business activities and how they did their strategic planning and financial reporting. Some of this information became very useful for the rest of my career.

I traveled to Switzerland on numerous occasions and learned how this multi-billion-dollar international corporation functioned. This was a real eye-opener!

Many European companies operate in business cartels, like the OPEC Oil Cartel. There was no entrepreneurism, and employees were afraid to make decisions or take actions that might backfire on them. Even relatively small decisions that we needed to make at our facility had to be approved by a management team in New York. It was no fun working for this multi-billion-dollar corporation.

Because of this merger, I gained a new appreciation for US technology and the Purdue engineers who worked at our company. All of us have heard the story of how the Swiss are leaders in precision technology. In fact, ***many Americans refer to the Swiss Watch as their definition of precision and technology excellence.*** Well, let me put this "Myth" to rest—

Landis & Gyr management was very upset that more than 5% of our electric meters required further calibration before they passed US quality inspection standards. So, they had us send 1,000 of our "failed" meters to Switzerland for review by Swiss engineers. They were then going to re-engineer our meters and get our company operating more efficiently—*like a Swiss Watch!* Well, guess what? Every one of our "failed" meters passed the international inspection standards that were used by the Swiss. Here was proof that the Purdue engineers who worked at our company had developed electric meters that were vastly superior to those of our international parent company.

During my years in West Lafayette, Indiana, I spent many days as a guest speaker in the engineering and business classrooms at Purdue University. I was thrilled that the professors and students wanted to incorporate entrepreneurism into their studies.

Purdue University has now established itself as having one of the most complete entrepreneurial programs in the world, and has become an incredible incubator for new business development—beginning with undergraduate engineering studies, followed by technology research and then by product development. These processes are then followed and supported by business entrepreneurship studies and business partnerships—thus giving Purdue graduates the complete package of technical and business backgrounds they need to become successful entrepreneurs.

Purdue leadership clearly recognizes that "Entrepreneurship" is much more than merely teaching a few business courses. In most instances good entrepreneurship programs are an integration of research, science, technology and business. Each facet contributes to the overall success of the project.

Other universities would do well to follow Purdue's approach for developing new businesses and our country's future entrepreneurs.

As mentioned earlier in this book, my wife and I continue to maintain close contacts with the wonderful administration and staff at Purdue and strongly support their cancer-research programs, which encourage participation from many different departments and technologies within the Purdue family.

I have never experienced this level of comprehensive study, internal cooperation, and vision at any other university. As stated earlier in this book—*good leadership doesn't just happen. It is the result of excellent strategic planning and step-by-step implementation by the visionary leaders and staff at Purdue.*

I know that some readers are wondering why I am such a big fan of Purdue. The reason is that I respect and greatly appreciate being around intelligent, successful people—and Purdue University is a great place to experience this environment.

Now, let's get back to the rest of my career with Duncan Electric Company and Landis & Gyr.

Three years after the takeover of Duncan Electric Company by Landis & Gyr, an Ohio engineering and manufacturing company that had been trying to recruit me for five years called again, as I was preparing for another trip to Switzerland.

The owner was getting ready to turn the leadership of his company over to his son (an Ivy League grad) and wanted me to reconsider and join the management team as their Vice President of Corporate Development. In this newly created position, I would get heavily involved with their international, manufacturing, and construction operations. Excellent! Now I had an opportunity to get back into an entrepreneurial company and make a difference.

This Big Corporation Lacked Entrepreneurism

Purdue Represents Entrepreneurism at Its Best

CHAPTER 36

International Business and Washington, DC

A s Corporate Development Officer of this mid-size Ohio engineering and manufacturing company, I was given the opportunity to define my own duties.

My position was a new concept for this company, which was dominated by mechanical, chemical, and electrical engineers, all of whom had extensive knowledge with the sciences that related to the various product lines that they designed, manufactured, and installed in domestic and international markets.

Many of these engineers and scientists were brilliant and had degrees from the finest engineering colleges in the United States. One was a Purdue engineering graduate. Another graduated with an engineering degree from MIT and had a Harvard MBA. *I loved this high-tech environment!* As this ole farm boy would say: *"I was in Hog Heaven!"*

This was another lengthy period of employment for me. I learned hands-on management of manufacturing operations, international business, and the financing of export sales. I also gained extensive exposure to the inner workings of many of the departments of our federal government, our Congress, and how lobbyists influence our government.

After three or four years with this firm, I got heavily involved with international sales and finance. I traveled throughout the world, including to Central and South America, the Middle East, several African Countries, Europe, and to China. During those years, we had to be invited by the central government of China and approved by our US State Department before we were allowed to travel to China.

Major career-changing events took place during my employment with this company, on a domestic and international scale. And, once again, I experienced some of the highest of the highs and lowest of the lows in my life.

Next

Facing Huge Challenges

CHAPTER 37

United States Congress and Export-Import Bank

B ecause our mid-size company was heavily involved with exports, I thoroughly studied the laws pertaining to our federal government's export programs at Wright State University (near Dayton, Ohio), which was a regional depository for federal-government documents. I was soon to discover that I knew more about our country's export laws than many of the political appointees who managed our federal government's agencies.

During the presidency of Ronald Reagan, the Director of the US Budget wanted to abolish the Export/Import Bank (EXIM) of the United States. He called it "Boeing's Bank," which was probably a fair characterization, since the majority of EXIM Bank's financing went to support the exports of 7 large US companies, including Boeing—while practically nothing went toward supporting exports from small and mid-size businesses.

Since more than one-third of our company's sales were exports, if the EXIM bank was abolished, our company would have been ruined. So, I called the offices of our US Senators and begged their staff to let me testify before the Senate Finance Committee that was going to hold hearings to reauthorize or to disband the EXIM Bank. *I got nowhere—and never got to speak with a Senator!*

So, I packed my bags, flew to Washington, DC, and started visiting the offices of every Senator who sat on the Senate Finance Committee. In every case I heard the same story—that the witness roster was full and the Senate Committee didn't need any more presentations. I then asked each senate staffer, "How many witnesses are from small businesses?" and they said "None." This is how I found an opening to testify—because no US Senator wanted to exclude small business from having a voice in this matter. Again, *during all of my begging at the US Senate offices—I never met or was introduced to a single United States Senator!*

I was shocked to learn that I was the only person in the United States from a small or medium-size business who was going to speak before the Senate Finance Committee regarding International Trade and Export Financing.

Getting to testify before the US Senate Finance Committee became a huge turning point in my career—for the good, for the bad, and for the ugly.

When I walked into the Senate hearing room, I was in awe of all of the reporters and TV cameras that filled the second-level balcony. I had never experienced anything like this. Clearly, these hearings were important to the news media.

Then, I saw my name at the end of the witness table that was positioned directly in front of the Senators, who were seated behind a beautiful crescent-shaped mahogany platform.

As I walked up to my seat, a security guard told me to step back, and that I would be called to the table after the President's men testified.

Remember, none of the Senators had ever met me before I was introduced to them that day. Then, after all of the President's men spoke, and as I moved to the table to deliver my statement, I heard a lot of noise coming from the second-level balcony. It was the news media disassembling their equipment, after hearing the President's men testify.

Well, it turned out that I was chosen as the buffer witness, while the media removed their cameras and audio equipment. Apparently, they were there solely to hear the President's men speak. Great! No one thought my testimony was going to be important. So, the news media was going to ignore me.

And, why should they listen to me? Just like our Senators, none of the media had ever met me or spoken to me. So, I changed my presentation by adding an opening statement—that I requested be kept off of the Senate Records.

Well, all of the Senators immediately looked up and took notice of this witness from small business—and the news media reacted quickly to see what was going to happen.

The Committee Chairman, Senator John Heinz from Pennsylvania, chose to withhold his ruling on my request to keep my opening comments off of the Senate's permanent records. He said that he would make a decision—after he heard my full testimony.

I then said, *"Senators, after hearing the President's men speak about how much they love to help small business promote their exports, I have just one thing to say, and that is—I haven't heard so much Bull since I was a young boy growing up on a small farm in Indiana."*

This was a shock to most of the Senators, who had no idea who this witness was from small business. I was lucky that they did not have the security guard immediately remove me from the chambers. Senator and Chairman John Heinz then asked, in a very stern voice, for me to explain myself—which I did.

I explained that the US Export/Import Bank was originally established in 1945 to protect US companies from losing export sales as a result of foreign governments using unfair trade practices, including subsidized financing, to secure exports from their countries.

Our United States Export-Import Bank was established to stop this unfair trade practice and to protect American jobs.

With the EXIM Bank, the United States had a tool by which it could neutralize foreign-government-subsidized financing, by offering the same subsidized-financing terms and conditions to the US exporter. By doing so, foreign governments lost their advantage, because they could no longer use this unfair trade practice to steal American exports and take jobs away from American workers.

I further stated that the Export/Import Bank was one of the most important jobs programs our government has ever had and that it would not cost US taxpayers a dime, if it functioned properly.

Why? The mere existence of this EXIM program was enough to prevent foreign governments from subsidizing the financing of their exports, because when they knew that the US exporter could obtain the same financing from the US government—their predatory-financing tactic became useless.

Therefore, as long as this program was in place at the EXIM Bank, our company never had to ask for subsidized financing, because no foreign government would initiate subsidized financing when they knew that we could match them and keep the manufacturing jobs here, in America.

When my testimony was finished, Senator Heinz asked me to explain why I didn't want my opening comments to appear on the Senate records. I said that I didn't want to embarrass the good Senator Lugar from my home state of Indiana. Mr. Heinz replied that my full testimony was going to be recorded in the United States Senate records, and that he and Senator Lugar agreed with everything I had to say.

Furthermore, Senator Heinz said that he was going to buy all of us a pair of hip boots, so that the next time we walked into the EXIM Bank, we wouldn't get our feet wet from all of that "Bull." As a member of the Republican Party, Senator Heinz could have stomped all over my opening statement. Instead, he chose to do the ethically and morally right thing—and recognize the honesty and accuracy of my testimony. *Senator Heinz was a Hero in my life.*

Needless to say, this testimony produced a tidal wave of news coverage and offers from the US Chamber of Commerce to become a Board Member of their Small Business Council, and participate in a number of national T.V. programs regarding international trade and small-business issues. I even appeared on the PBS MacNeil/Lehrer television program with Dr. Martin Feldstein (President Reagan's Chief Economic Advisor) regarding the manipulation of currencies by foreign governments, and other unfair international trade practices.

It's amazing that, to this day, our national leaders still have not stopped many of the unfair trade practices that are used by foreign governments. The United States has incurred trade deficits for nearly all of the last fifty years. This has resulted in the loss of millions of American jobs. "Free Trade" is worthless, unless it is "Fair" to all participating countries. It's time for America to wake up and demand "Fair Trade," not the phony concept of "Free Trade" that has been abused by many foreign countries.

I then became a regular author of international business articles for both the US Chamber's nationally distributed *Outlook* magazine and the *Enterprise* magazine, which was published by the National Association of Manufacturers.

The National Association of Manufacturers put me on their International Policy Committee, and the NFIB (National Federation of Independent Businesses) incorporated my experiences and ideas in their national radio programs. The *Wall Street Journal* and *Nation's Business* also wrote articles concerning my activities in our nation's capital.

This series of events helped me develop a great relationship with senior management at the US Department of Commerce and attracted the attention of our Secretary of Commerce, Malcolm Baldrige. It turned out that Secretary Baldrige was on my side and fully understood the damage that would be done to American exports and American jobs if we no longer had the EXIM Bank.

You see, if the EXIM Bank had been abolished, then foreign governments would have had an unfettered opportunity to steal export sales from American companies by offering subsidized financing to support exports from their countries. This would have resulted in the loss of millions of additional American manufacturing jobs.

Only one leader from big business was outspoken in support of my initiatives for small business at the EXIM Bank. That man was Donald M. Kendall, the President of PepsiCo. He was also the Chairman of the Board for the US Chamber of Commerce.

I will never forget my meeting before the Executive Committee of the US Chamber's Board. At that meeting, I had only one supporter on my side from the US Chamber (Ivan Elmer), while all of the big-business representatives and the US Chamber's attorneys sat at the other end of the table, trying to stop my EXIM bank initiative that would establish a budget set-aside, to be used exclusively to support export programs for small and medium-size businesses.

Why was a set-aside necessary? The answer was simple. We proved that the EXIM Bank couldn't document that a single percent of their budget was used to support exports from small businesses—even though small businesses employed more than 73% of the US workforce. Nearly their entire budget was used to support exports from a few large companies—as Mr. Stockman, the President's Budget Director, correctly stated. So, without a mandate from the US Senate, there was no reason to believe that EXIM Bank leadership would change the way they conducted their business activities in the future.

After hearing both sides of the debate, Mr. Kendall spoke up and said that big business and the Chamber's attorneys did not understand the challenges facing small business, and that they were nothing but "Pigs at the Trough, who wanted everything for themselves and wanted to exclude small business from participating in the international marketplace." He then took a vote, in which the Executive Committee of the Board chose to unanimously support my small-business initiative.

Mr. Kendall then instructed the President of the US Chamber to call the White House and inform President Reagan that the US Chamber would not support Mr. Stockman's position for eliminating the EXIM Bank, because it was a very important program that protected the jobs of American workers and promoted growth for US companies, including small businesses.

Don, thank you for your integrity, and thank you for standing up for the best interest of small business and the American workers they employ.

To me, Don Kendall and Ivan Elmer are Heroes. They both did what was morally right and what was in the best interest of American workers.

In the end, we had every important business association and labor union in the United States supporting our position, and we succeeded in getting both Houses of Congress to reauthorize the charter of the EXIM Bank, with the first-ever mandated set-aside, to be used exclusively to support small-business exports.

In the past, the US Chamber of Commerce had supported the concept of "survival of the fittest." But, in this situation, the US Chamber and our Congress knew that small business had little or no chance of succeeding in export markets unless the EXIM Bank had a mandate to actively provide support—which it routinely gave to big business.

Who would have thought that this small-town Hoagland, Indiana farm boy could go to Washington, DC, and convince a bureaucratic Congress to pass legislation that would give small businesses a real opportunity to succeed in the international marketplace—and save the jobs of millions of American workers?

During this time, I became a very good friend to Florida Congressman Andy Ireland, who was Chairman of the House Small Business Committee. He was a wonderful, honest, and hard-working elected official who made sure that government bureaucrats did not prevail on this important jobs issue. I will have more to say about Congressman Ireland a bit later in this book.

President Reagan then began to extol the virtues of the EXIM Bank and what an important program it was to preserve and grow jobs for American workers.

One other special event took place during this time. I had the pleasure of finally meeting with Ohio Senator and astronaut John Glenn. And yes, *I was "Spaced-Out"* by this opportunity to sit down and chat with an American Hero who had truly been *"Out of this World."*

By the way, Senator Glenn never found time to meet with me—until after he heard about the impact my testimony had on the Senate Finance Committee.

From this experience, I learned just how hard it is for the "little guy" to be heard by our elected representatives in Washington, DC. Unfortunately, the small-business owners and individuals like you and me, who elect these people to represent us in Washington, DC, really have little contact with or impact on these folks once they are elected, that is—until they need our vote to remain in office.

I would be remiss if I did not pass on several other important experiences that I had with our government. First, I always thought that our Congressmen and Senators wrote the legislation that they enacted. I no longer believe this. My experience was that it was their staff who drafted the legislation—with considerable influence from special-interest groups and lobbyists, who frequently met with the staff. Those lobbyists wanted to make sure that their companies' specific wants and desires were incorporated into the newly drafted legislation.

Second, because of all of the past news reports concerning our elected officials being influenced by free drinks, meals, etc., I was shocked to find that it was their staff who regularly got wined and dined at the local restaurants and pubs that surround the House and Senate office buildings. In fact, at the end of one of my days in a congressman's office, a staffer invited me to join her at an Irish Pub to have free hors d'oeuvres and drinks with lobbyists. I learned that this was a "networking" opportunity for staffers—to look for their next job with a business association, or as a lobbyist for a big corporation, should their boss not get re-elected to office. These folks really stuck together and protected each other—much like the "Deep-State" that we hear about in today's news.

Third, I will never forget one female staffer who lamented the fact that she had made a huge mistake when she took a job in Washington, DC, for her US Senator, shortly after graduating college. She had worked in Washington, DC, for more than seven years—and just realized that she had failed to gain the work experience she needed to return to her home state of Iowa and obtain a comparable-paying job. As a result, she felt that she was a prisoner to the Washington, DC, governmental environment, with little hope of changing her career path or returning to her home state of Iowa.

Please remember my earlier comment—"the first job a person takes after college is one of the most important career decisions they will make in their life." Unfortunately, the first job this young woman took following college proved to be a disaster for her career—and for her personally. So, please take heed!

Now, having said this, I am sure that few if any elected officials or their staff will admit that the foregoing is common practice. But—that was my real-world experience in Washington, DC, and I believe it represents the real world in which we live.

There Was More to Come

CHAPTER 38

Mexico's Financial Crisis

The second major event that took place with this Ohio company pertained to the economic crisis that happened in Mexico during the mid-1980s. During that time, Mexico cut off imports from the United States and required US companies to have manufacturing operations in Mexico. Further, Mexico required that all new foreign companies have a 51% Mexican owner, who would have decision-making control over the Mexican operation(s).

This was a crushing blow to our company, since Mexico was the destination for many of our exports, and, as an engineering company, we could not risk losing control over our intellectual property, engineering drawings, and unique manufacturing processes to a 51% foreign owner. Therefore, the only way we could avoid employee layoffs was to obtain approval from the Mexican government to establish a wholly owned US subsidiary in Mexico—something the Mexican government no longer allowed.

Well, guess what? Neither the 3rd-generation owner of our company nor any of the other officers wanted to tackle this huge problem. So, again, the problem was assigned to me. Mexico soon became my home-away-from-home.

During the next 12 months, I convinced Mexico's Secretary of Commerce (Hector Hernandez) and its Foreign Investment Commission Chairman (Adolfo Hegewisch) that small-business investment in Mexico would be a huge positive for their country, for many reasons.

First, no small business was going to move in and take over a town, as large foreign companies had done in the past. Second, recruiting small businesses would help create a broader manufacturing base in Mexico that would provide for a more stable economy and serve as an export base for Mexican products.

From these discussions, I was able to negotiate for two wholly owned US subsidiaries in Mexico. This was accomplished without paying any bribes or making any commitments to those who approved our requests. In doing so, we became the only company from the United States to be granted this type of foreign-investment approval. By the way, at that time, business bribes were a common practice in Mexico.

During my career, I experienced a tremendous amount of graft and financial corruption through the world. Unfortunately, it is more prevalent than we might think or want to believe. But, those are not my morals, ethics, or values—and I sincerely hope that you will practice similar good morals, ethics, and values during your career!

From the above, a reader might infer that this was a relatively easy task. In fact, it was a very difficult task—otherwise many other US companies would have succeeded with their request for 100% foreign ownership in Mexico. I cannot begin to describe the maze of government corruption I had to navigate.

Our company's approval was so significant that Secretary of Commerce Malcolm Baldrige held a meeting to congratulate me for this tremendous success.

During my negotiations, I had numerous meetings in Mexico City with John Glavin, the US Ambassador to Mexico, and Calvin Berlin, the Commercial Attaché. After retiring from service with our federal government, Mr. Berlin taught at the Miller College of Business at Ball State University.

It was during this time that Ball State had me speak and mentor their students and staff concerning International Business—after which the University established an International Business major. I strongly encouraged that this course of study result in a "minor" (not a major) in International Business, which it is today. Why? The answer is fairly simple—companies generally do not hire people to start their career in International Business. Instead, they hire people with degrees in finance, accounting, engineering, etc. Those new employees then learn and grow into the international operations of the business.

Therefore, having a "minor" in International Business is a significant plus—but it is rarely the primary reason for landing a student's first job after they graduate college.

So, sometimes good things happen to honest people—even to a small-town farm boy from Hoagland, Indiana.

Again, ethics and values matter. My good reputation was invaluable—so was my persistence and refusal to give in to failure!

Tough Challenges Can Be Overcome
With Knowledge, Honesty, and Integrity

CHAPTER 39

Recognition

As a result of my initiatives before Congress regarding reauthorization of the EXIM Bank, my other legislative involvements regarding Domestic International Sales Corporations (DISC), small-business taxation, and our success in working with the governments of China, Egypt, the Sudan, and Mexico, a number of very nice surprises came my way. None were expected. I thought that I was just doing my job.

First came respect and recognition from Florida's Congressman Andy Ireland, who was Chairman of the House Small Business Committee. He was a very kind, dedicated, and special man.

When the Chairman of the EXIM Bank started attacking my public testimony, Mr. Ireland invited the Bank's Chairman to debate with me before the House Small Business Committee. In doing so, the House Small Business Committee quickly saw the knowledge, honesty, and integrity behind my testimony. The Chairman of the EXIM Bank left that hearing with his tail dragging on the floor.

Congressman Ireland thanked me profusely for the contribution I made to the US economy. He then signed a picture of himself, in gold ink, stating: *"To Evan. If people only knew the good you have accomplished. Andy."*

May Congressman Ireland rest in peace. He was a very caring and special person, who represented the very best of morals, ethics and values among our elected officials. He was a hero in my life.

Then, President Reagan invited me and the US Chamber's Small Business Council to join him for breakfast at the Mayflower Hotel, across from the White House. President Reagan was a strong advocate for small business, and encouraged everyone to pursue their American Dream.

Secretary of Commerce Malcolm Baldrige appointed me to be his Program Chairman for the first National District Export Council Conference, held in Washington, DC. This was a huge honor, because it came from a government official I greatly respected, who also had good morals, ethics, and values.

In addition, Secretary Baldrige honored my service by awarding our company the prestigious "President's E-Award" for Excellence in Exporting. Prior to my involvement in Washington, DC, I was unaware that this recognition even existed. I was too busy solving problems and building our business, and never sought recognition for doing my job.

The governor of Ohio then appointed me to become his advisor and member of the Ohio Trade Council.

The US Chamber of Commerce in Washington, DC nominated me to be recognized as the "United States Small Business Exporter of the Year," a recognition that was bestowed by the US Small Business Administration. Wow, I had no idea that such an honor existed. I was merely trying to do what was in the best interest of our country and my company. So, this recognition came as a huge surprise to me.

Now, for some Bad News. My company was now run by a 3rd-generation Ivy League College graduate, who was born and raised with a silver spoon in his mouth. He truly believed the world revolved around him. Upon learning that the US Chamber had nominated me for this national recognition, he threw a tantrum and insisted that his name be included in the application. He rationalized that I would never have achieved my level of success had he and his dad not hired me. Therefore, anything that I accomplished (anywhere in the world) was due to his brilliant leadership—because it was he and his dad who had hired me!

Well, recognition is not something that I have ever sought for myself, so I had the folks who prepared the documents for the Small Business Administration revise the application to include the name of our company's owner, so that he would share this prestigious recognition with me. He then provided the documentation to support his worthiness for this national recognition.

Well, guess what? After reading the application, the US Small Business Administration concluded that our company's owner had done nothing to deserve the recognition—and removed his name from the application.

Normally, when the SBA makes this kind of major alteration, the application is removed from further consideration. However, rather than disqualifying the entire application, the SBA gave me the honor of "Ohio Exporter of the Year," and "Runner-up" to the United States Exporter of the Year. The owner of our company received nothing—not even a letter of appreciation.

Now, as you can imagine, the foregoing caused a rather unpleasant atmosphere to develop at our company. The owner would not even allow the Small Business Administration officials to visit our plant for the presentations and associated photo-op relating to these prestigious awards and recognition.

Instead, I took a day of vacation and quietly drove to Columbus, Ohio, where the award presentations were made. And, no—I never displayed any of those national recognitions in my office at the Ohio Company. I keep them in my closet, at home.

Now that I am retired, I am looking at them in my home office, as I write this book. They bring back a lot of good, and some not-so-pleasant memories.

Well, it was obvious that the more I accomplished with this company, the more jealous the owner became—even though these accomplishments were putting money in his pocket! It was clear that it was going to be difficult to maintain a pleasant working relationship with this 3rd-generation family owner.

Looking back on life, I learned that this is not an unusual experience with a 2nd- or 3rd-generation business owner who never took a business risk or shed their own blood, sweat and tears to build a business. It was his daddy or granddad who paid the price for success. Now you can better understand why I consider many of these 2nd- and 3rd-generation business owners to be "spoiled brats," who were born and raised with a "silver spoon in their mouth," and then inherited daddy's business—without "Paying the Price for Success."

Having said this, I am pleased to say that, until this time, when national recognition and awards came my way, I had a wonderful experience with this company, and greatly appreciated working among its team of engineers.

In addition to working with these talented engineers, I got extensive, in-depth experience with various departments of our federal government, and traveled throughout the world.

In doing so, I saw the Great Pyramids of Egypt, the National Museum of Egypt with the King Tut Exhibit, the Valley of the Kings, the Nile River, the Aswan Dam, and the palaces of King Tut and Anthony and Cleopatra, and her in-ground swimming pool. These were wonderful experiences!

I walked on the Great Wall of China during my travels and visited the ancient gold museum of Bogota, Colombia, which contains the largest exhibit of indigenous gold artifacts in the world—absolutely beautiful! But I must tell you, walking the sidewalks of Bogota was very dangerous, because of thieves and muggers. So, I never walked alone in this city.

I was fortunate to visit many of the great art museums of Europe and attended live-theater productions in London, including "*Cats*"—*Absolutely Wonderful!* Prior to this, the only cats this farm boy had ever seen were the cats that kept the mice and rats out of the barn on our small family farm.

Many of my travels were to developing countries. During one of my trips to China, a young woman who was an Undersecretary of Commerce accompanied us throughout our trip. During the trip, she asked many questions and got to know us quite well. Near the end of our trip, while sitting in an airport to board our flight home, I noticed that she was crying. I worried that I had said something wrong or had offended her. Then, she told me that the reason she was crying was because she knew that she would never be able to live the "American Dream." She stated that the government controlled her life, including where she worked and where she lived. She was sad that she would never have the freedom and opportunities that we enjoy in the United States.

Several years later, we learned that spies from the Chinese Government had followed us during our trip. Apparently while local leaders from various cities entertained us during the evenings, these spies copied the engineering drawings that our sales engineer had brought with him. We learned of this when China soon began making those specific products—without any help from our staff. Of course, the Chinese versions failed, because they did not understand our unique manufacturing processes that hardened our steel.

I also visited some very dangerous countries, and saw hoodlums descend from mountains and attack villages—including in Mexico. These are memories, but I can assure you they are not highlights of my international travels. However, they do remind me of why I am so grateful to have been born in the United States of America, where we have an opportunity to achieve nearly anything we can dream—if we are willing to pay the price to achieve our dreams.

Last, when traveling internationally, it was important to respect the dining customs and practices of local residents, so we didn't offend our foreign hosts. When possible, we always ate at least some of the cuisine and food delicacies that were provided. Sometimes this was very challenging!

For instance, when traveling in China, on several occasions we were served meals that included shark intestines. Also included was a fish, with its head fully attached. We were expected to suck the eyeballs out of the fish head, and eat them—Wow! I must admit, that I couldn't and didn't touch the fish eyes.

When in Egypt, one host provided us with a meat dish that had been sitting on the table for quite some time and was covered with flies. To avoid getting sick while eating this food, we cut off the top layers of the meat, and ate the remainder.

In the Sudan (Africa), we were guests at a gathering where the main appetizer was marinated, uncooked goat lungs—Wow! One little bite proved that the lungs had no taste, other than the marinating sauce. Second, chewing a piece of goat lungs was like trying to eat a piece of synthetic sponge that can be purchased at any grocery or retail store in the United States. In short, it was so tough that it was impossible to eat. But, we had to put on a pleasant face and smile, because our host had purchased this goat specifically for this occasion. Oh, the main course at this gathering was baked pigeon—with its head still attached—Yummy!

As I have said before, and will say again—

We are truly fortunate to be citizens of this wonderful country we call the United States of America!

These Were Primarily

Positive Memories from My Life

CHAPTER 40

Swimming With The Sharks

My national exposure with this Ohio Company resulted in other firms wanting to hire me as their President. One was a private equity firm in New York, whose primary owner was a friend of Malcolm Baldrige, our Secretary of Commerce.

Prior to owning his private-equity firm, this person was President Richard Nixon's appointee to run the Overseas Private Investment Corporation (OPIC) in Washington, DC. Its purpose is to help US companies establish joint ventures in foreign countries.

After an initial interview at his palatial home on a private lake in New York, I was quickly hired to take over as president of a struggling company that his firm had acquired in Toledo, Ohio.

The 3rd-generation owner of the Ohio engineering and manufacturing company was determined not to lose me. He said: "Evan, you are not leaving. Everyone has their price. What is yours?"

I told him that I was not leaving for money, but to become the president of a company, with the hope of building it into a larger firm that would eventually be taken public. I was not for sale! As I said earlier in this book: "Money does not buy happiness." But, the money will be there the more we succeed in our career.

Now, in regard to this private-equity firm, I love to ask high school and college students how many of them enjoy watching *Shark Tank* on TV. As it turns out, many students enjoy watching the "Sharks," as they ask questions and attack (challenge) the entrepreneurial presenters.

Well, my real-life experience taught me that *the Sharks on "Shark Tank" are* really quite nice, even Mr. Wonderful. In fact, they are *"Pussy Cats" who purr.*

The private-equity firm I joined represented the real world of "Sharks." They financially leveraged my new company to the maximum extent possible, were raking off an annual management fee for themselves, and expected me to quadruple their money within a few years—the faster the better. And, they didn't care how I got the job done. Oh—and they considered employees to be nothing more than an expense. They were greedy for money, money, money—and it seemed that nothing else mattered to them! *Where was Mr. Wonderful when I needed him?* He was so much nicer then the Sharks I had to swim with.

During the 1980s, this type of leveraged buyout was common in many industries. A number of news organizations reported on some of the abuses of this type of high-leverage financing, including the bankruptcy of Diamond-Bathurst in the glass bottling industry. It was a consolidation of multiple failing glass bottle manufacturing operations into a single company, which was then sold to the public. Guess what? Diamond-Bathurst soon became one of the largest bankruptcies in the glass industry. But, the leveraged-buyout people got their money, when they sold the company to the public! Some of those guys sat on my company's Board of Directors. Yep, I was truly swimming with the sharks!

Interestingly, this Toledo, Ohio company had also been owned by a 2nd-generation family member, who was born and raised with a "silver spoon" in his mouth, educated at an Ivy League College, belonged to a fancy country club, and thought that he was the smartest guy in Ohio—and beyond.

It was only later that I learned that the main reason the private-equity firm purchased this company was because both owners had established a close friendship during their college days and were still fishing buddies.

The bottom line was that I had just walked into a political nightmare. This 2nd-generation owner remained in the company, as an "advisor." Since I had already purchased a new home in Toledo, it was time to make the best of it, get down to work, and strategize on how to rebuild this failing business.

The company was a high-volume manufacturer of glass shelving and windows for refrigerators, stoves and other appliances, a wholesale distributor of glass, and owner of three commercial construction companies. None of these divisions had any common markets or internal synergies, and no one had ever developed a strategic plan for the company's future. All of these divergent operations had been started and built by the father, who was a serial entrepreneur.

Early on, I sold the wholesale distribution and construction companies to the local managers who were already in charge of those operations. They were thrilled to have their own operation—and believe me, they were very happy to get away from the New York private-equity company.

Now, I had to figure out how to transform the core business, which was commodity glass manufacturing, into a viable growth-company, or consolidate it with other companies, so the owners could take it public through an IPO (Initial Public Offering). This division had manufacturing operations in Ohio and in Texas. Together they served all US markets, except the West Coast.

I was leery of consolidations with similar companies. Bigger is not always better, especially for commodity products. And, through research, I had learned about the large bankruptcy of Diamond-Bathurst, so I was very skeptical of initiating another consolidation of this type.

Now, having said this, I must state that the Board was very much in favor of consolidations with other companies—because they had apparently made a lot of money with the Diamond-Bathurst consolidations and their IPO, when they took this company public. *To them it was all about $$—money!*

Since most of my experience had been with technology-driven companies, I felt that it was best to rebuild this company with the infusion of new technology.

Fortunately, while living in Ohio, I became friends with a gentleman named Harold McMaster, who was a wonderful human being and a brilliant physicist. Harold invented and patented the machines that formed the curved window glass for automobiles. Through his company, Harold built the equipment that was sold worldwide to major automotive and glass-manufacturing companies. He had a monopoly on this business, because of the many patents that he held.

Unfortunately, as a child, Harold contracted polio and was physically challenged. But, he had a brilliant mind, and we loved discussing how to re-envision and evolve both of our companies. Harold and I were similar in many respects—including the fact that both of us lived very simple lives, neither of us had ever laid off a single employee during our career, and both of us had created many new jobs—thus enriching the lives of others and their families. *Harold McMaster was my "Stephen Hawking" of physics,* and a wonderful inspiration in my life. Over many cups of coffee (I love coffee), we discussed how to transform my company into a technology-driven business. Well, my friend Harold was deeply interested in solar power. The facilities and equipment that I had in my new company would be a good fit for the manufacture of solar panels. The only problem was that neither of us had any connections with companies that produced photo-voltaic cells, which are the heart of solar-panel technology.

Therefore, I began researching the photo-voltaic industry in the United States and found a company that was located in our area, not too far from Chicago, Illinois. This firm was run by two brothers who were engineers, but had no money to build a production facility. So, during my third year with the private-equity firm, I convinced the owners of this photo-voltaic engineering company to merge with our company, and we would focus on becoming a national leader in solar-panel energy generation. That was the Good News.

Now, for the Bad News. Unbeknownst to me, while I was coordinating merger negotiations with my private-equity company and the Illinois firm, the two brothers were negotiating directly with my private-equity company. They wanted to end up as the senior management team, following the merger of our two companies.

I'm sure that everyone reading this book understands what this meant. *Ouch!*

Well, on a Friday, during my third year with this private-equity firm, I was visited by a representative from their headquarters. He informed me that my services were no longer needed and that my employment was terminated—effective immediately.

On the following Monday, the merger was announced, and everyone on the management team (that I left behind) thought they were in seventh heaven, that they were going to become part of a national solar-panel empire—and that they were all going to get rich! At least that is the way management from the private-equity company portrayed the merger to the management team that I had built.

As I stated earlier, once a person leaves their place of employment—they are quickly forgotten and become as undesirable as the stale bagels left over from yesterday's breakfast buffet. I quickly learned that *I was now the stale bagel!*

Another old adage is: "What goes around comes around."

So, here was a newly consolidated management team whose members were out to benefit themselves—just like the management from the private-equity company! They could see the dollar signs in their eyes; they were all going to get rich! But, who could they trust?

The engineering brothers did not trust the private-equity firm, so they did not allow anyone (other than themselves) to have access to or understand the science behind their photo-voltaic technology. This led to a very messy situation, which (you guessed it) led to a failing company that dissolved within five years. All of the employees lost their jobs. And, none of the members of the greedy management team got rich! Again folks, *morals, values, and ethics really do count in this life. At least, I thought they did.*

Management greed caused this business failure. This is another lesson we learn (the hard way) during our lifetime. As the old adage states: "Birds of a feather flock together." These birds were alike—all were out for themselves. In the end, they got exactly what they deserved, because they were all out of a job and had to start over with their careers. Unfortunately, those greedy birds hurt a lot of innocent workers and their families along the way—because those good workers lost their jobs.

The only pleasant experience that I had while swimming with the sharks was that I had lunch with President George Herbert Walker Bush, a former classmate of one of the individuals associated with the private-equity firm. Mr. Bush seemed to be a kindhearted man—unlike the sharks at the private-equity company. Like President Reagan, President Bush had a deep and profound love for our constitutional liberties that not only allow, but encourage every citizen to pursue their own American Dream.

I also traveled to Berne, Switzerland, where the private-equity company held its annual meeting with its worldwide investors. I have never experienced such a display of wealth and garish behavior in my life. And, I never want to experience it again! This meeting was a lavish party that did not represent the values, morals, or ethics that defined my childhood or my adult life.

So, as you can see, a number of people took advantage of this small-town farm boy during his career. But, in the end, they were the ones who failed!

It's called ego and greed. I have never taken credit or benefited from someone else's hard work—and these folks failed (miserably) when they abused their positions of authority and tried to benefit from the leadership that I brought to their failing company.

Where are the good morals, values, and ethics that I was taught to cherish while being raised on a farm in Hoagland, Indiana? Have they ever existed? Or, am I just one of the most naïve small-town farm boys you have ever known?

And, I can tell you from experience that it really hurt to get pushed off of the wagon, after all of the hard work had been completed—just so someone else could step in and try to reap the benefits that resulted from my hard work.

As a follow-up to this section, I am pleased to let you know that my good friend Harold McMaster went on to develop his own solar-cell technology, and founded Glasstech Solar in 1984, followed by Solar Cells, Inc. By the time of his passing in 2003, my dear friend Harold had been issued more than 100 patents. I thank God for bringing Harold McMaster into my life. Harold was a major hero to me, because he strengthened my passion for pursuing and integrating new technology into every company I managed. Harold was a scientific genius! May he, too, rest in peace.

Life Is Not Always Fair

But, Did I Learn from This Experience?

CHAPTER 41

Trust Me

Soon after my door closed with the private-equity company, several other doors quickly opened. In one instance, a large international CPA firm had a client in the Indianapolis area that was failing and hadn't made a profit for approximately six years. It produced and sold farm and commercial grain dryers. The company hadn't sold a single commercial grain dryer in more than four years, and was now limited to selling large blowers, fans, and farm dryers.

This was also a 2nd-generation family-owned company. The owner wanted to sell badly, because he was elderly, in ill health—and was losing his shirt with his failing business. Therefore, we drafted a contract that allowed me to buy the company at a predetermined price, if I got the company back on its feet. The predetermined price was the audited value of the company on the day that I stepped in as president.

Wow, what an opportunity, to own a grain-dryer manufacturing company! Heck, when growing up on our small farm, we were so poor that we never dreamed of owning a grain dryer. Now, I had an opportunity to own a company that manufactured these machines—if I succeeded in turning it around.

Then, the partner from the CPA firm requested that I agree to one *"minor"* change in my employment contract that would read (paraphrase):

> *"Evan can buy 49% of the company any time he wishes, but if he buys more than 49%, he then must buy it all (100%)."*

This change was made because the company had a $6 million tax-loss carry-forward, much of which would have been lost if I had a written option to purchase more than 49% of the company—according to IRS tax regulations.

However, with this *"minor"* change in my contract, everyone would benefit because the company would not have to pay any federal income tax on the first $6 million of profits that my leadership produced—that is, if I was successful in turning around this failing company. Remember, the company had not been profitable for any of the past six years!

I trusted the owner and his financial and legal team, since everyone knew that the owner, who was very religious, was ill and wanted to sell. *After all, if I couldn't trust these professionals and the religious owner, who could I trust?*

So, I accepted this *"minor"* change, since it was in the best interest of the current owner, and presumably would not have a negative impact on me.

I was soon going to learn that trusting another 2nd-generation family-owner who had run his company into the ground was a huge mistake!

I should have listened to President Ronald Reagan when he said that he trusted everyone, but that he would always insist on having a way to "verify." His phrase "Trust, But Verify" meant that he trusted no one. President Reagan understood human nature, and had clearly learned from his prior experiences. As you will soon read, this Hoagland farm boy had not yet learned this lesson.

Well, the first thing I did was make peace with the union employees who had not received a wage increase for years. I let them know the business was failing, and that we were either going to succeed together, or we were all going to fail together and lose our jobs. Unlike many management/labor relations we read about, this group of employees and I got along great, and they defended me before their outside union bosses. As a team, we were going to save this company—if it was possible.

While studying the management team, I learned that our company no longer held any patents on its designs or processes. And, this same management team had allowed a large competitor to reverse-engineer our dryers, advertise them as "the same as" our dryers, and sell them at a lower price, without taking any legal action to stop the competitor.

So, there I was again, with a company that was making what was essentially a commodity product. I had to find a way to differentiate our company from everyone else in the industry. Equally bad, this company had not sold a single commercial grain dryer to the large grain elevators during the past four years—meaning that we had totally lost this major segment of the grain-dryer market.

Our professional engineers had retired on-the-job and were doing nothing but collecting a paycheck, while supporting the status quo.

I quickly learned that Zimmerman, an Illinois Company, was the leading manufacturer of commercial grain dryers in the United States. My research determined that this company was owned by a private-equity company in Chicago, whose primary business was in the leasing of aircraft. Immediately, I questioned why an airplane-leasing company would want to own a grain-dryer manufacturing company.

So, I called the Chicago private-equity company and set up an appointment to meet with their president. To make a long story short, during my second year with this company, the Chicago private-equity firm agreed to sell their Zimmerman grain-dryer company to us, in exchange for a five-year promissory note, with no cash down. They really wanted to get rid of this company, since it had no synergism with their core business. It seemed as though I was doing them a favor by taking Zimmerman off of their hands.

This move immediately propelled my company into the leadership position in the commercial segment of the grain-dryer industry.

Surprisingly, the 2nd-generation family owner of my company said nothing to me. No "Congratulations"—nothing! But, I must tell my readers that this was a typical reaction that I experienced from 2nd-generation family owners, who go through life believing that life is "All About Them!" I have yet to meet a 2nd- or 3rd-generation family owner who ever gave other people credit for successes that happened within their business.

In addition to making peace with the union employees and buying the Zimmerman commercial grain-dryer company, I joined the Venture Club of Indiana and an engineering club in Indianapolis. I spent a great deal of time having weekend coffees with several of those engineers.

One of the engineers turned out to be the genius who developed the first battery for the IBM Personal Computer. He was a darn good scientist—but a horrible businessman. During a visit to his laboratory (his garage), I learned that he also experimented with "fish finders" for weekend fishermen. As we exchanged experiences, I learned that fish finders use "sonar" technology, which sends a signal out into the water, and when the signal hits an object that is denser than water, it sends a response back to the receiver.

Over time, I questioned this engineer as to whether he might be able to modify the traditional use of sonar technology, so we could establish a "standard" density for properly dried grain at harvest time. You see, if a farmer sells his grain to the elevator when it is too wet, he gets "docked" and receives a lower price. He loses money! So, farmers typically over-dry their grain in their farm dryers, to make sure they don't get docked by the elevator. This creates another problem, because when the farmer over-dries his grain, he still loses money, because he has shrunk his crop and has less volume of grain to sell.

Well, this engineer and I worked together until we developed sonar technology for our dryers. It was so successful that it allowed us to market a grain dryer that could pay for itself during its first year of operation, by making sure that users neither under-dried nor over-dried their grain.

The year our new technology hit the market, we sold every commercial grain dryer in the United States, but one. And, from improved profitability, I was able to fully pay for the Zimmerman acquisition during our second year of ownership.

The farm market for our sonar grain dryers was just as hot, and we quickly built a multi-year backlog, because everyone wanted our new technology. Why? Because we were providing American farmers with a technology that made their lives better and more productive, and we did it at a price that allowed the user to pay for their new grain dryer during its first year of operation. *Remember, people and customers reward you and me—based on how we improve their lives, and not what's in it for us.*

Additionally, during my early years with this company, we entered the international marketplace and grew at a phenomenal rate.

As a result of our acquisition of Zimmerman, developments in new technology, our very successful move into international markets, and my leadership as the Chairman of the Indiana District Export Council, the US Department of Commerce nominated my company for the "President's E Award," for Excellence in Exporting.

At that time, through an Indianapolis investment banking firm, I secured funds to pay cash for 100% of the company, in accordance with the purchase price that was defined in my contract.

Then, this trusting farm boy got hit with another dose of real-life experiences, and the cruelty that humans can inflict on each other.

When I met with the 2nd-generation family owner and his attorney, with a check for the total purchase price of $15 million to buy the company, I was surprised to see the partner from the CPA firm also in attendance—and felt as though something was not right.

I was then informed that the owner would indeed sell me 49% of the company, but that my contract did not state that I had a **"right"** to buy 100% of the company. It merely stated that **"if"** I bought more than 49%, I then must buy it all. But, it did not state that the owner had to sell me more than 49%.

Apparently, the professional firms working with (and for) the company knew exactly what was going to happen—but they were more concerned with protecting their legal, audit, tax, and banking businesses than doing what was morally and ethically right.

I was then informed that my services were terminated, that the owner was going to keep his company and would not be selling it to me. However, they assured me that I could still give them cash for up to 49% of the ownership—per my contract. Now, everyone knows that the person who owns 51% of the company has total control. So, my having 49% ownership was essentially the same as having zero control.

Wow, two 2nd-generation business turnarounds in succession! Each time I was pushed off the hay wagon, after achieving success, while the owners who ran the company into the ground got rewarded. *So much for "Trust Me."*

The company's banker acknowledged that he was not surprised, because this type of action was typical of the owner's past actions. The banker further stated that he would have told me what was going to happen but wanted to protect the interest of his bank. He was very happy that I was successful in rebuilding this failing company, because it assured everyone that his bank would be fully repaid for the $3.6 million of loans it had made to the company—all borrowed by the 2nd-generation owner, prior to my arrival. I never borrowed a dime while rebuilding this company—except for the Zimmerman acquisition, which was not a "loan" but a debt instrument that was totally paid off within two years.

So much for the morals, ethics, and integrity of this highly religious owner, his international CPA firm, his lawyer, and his banker! Now you can better understand why I am not sure that the morals, ethics, and values of older generations were any better than today's morals, ethics, and values. And remember, it is from older generations that younger generations learn their morals, ethics, and values. So, adults should practice what they preach—otherwise, how can they expect future generations to conduct themselves differently, when they see their elders lying, cheating, and being immoral?

Again, *what happened to the good morals and values that I was taught to respect during my childhood? Have they ever existed?* Or, was I duped by adults and by the leaders of the church that we attended? *What do you think?*

I will never trust another person who wears his/her religion on their sleeve and tells me that I can "trust" them because of their religion. I got burned twice. I have also learned my lesson about "trusting" 2nd-generation family owners.

The week of my termination, I attended the dinner, held by the US Department of Commerce, where I formally received the "President's E Award," for Excellence in Exporting. Upon receiving this award, I became the first business leader in the United States to receive the "President's E Award" for Excellence in Exporting, for two different companies, in different industries.

Can you imagine how demoralized and betrayed I felt, attending that dinner to receive a national award—after I had just been fired? No words can begin to express the betrayal I felt at that time. I never realized that it was humanly possible to feel that low.

But—*I never gave up on myself, and I never quit on myself,* as you will soon learn.

President Reagan, I Now Understand Your Statement— "Trust, But Verify"

CHAPTER 42

Experience Leads To Success

(Said the Great Guru)

t's not that I didn't achieve success in my career up to this point in time, but it seemed that, the more I succeeded in turning around and rebuilding someone else's company, the more I got stabbed in the back or stomped on, due to greed, big egos, or for other reasons. Maybe this is the reason the young lady with the Harvard MBA did not want to follow in my footsteps, after I shared my career experiences with her. As stated earlier in this book—she chose to pursue a different career path.

Having been taken advantage of by owner after owner, I was determined to never again take on the responsibility of turning around someone else's company, unless I had an ironclad agreement to own that company, if and when I succeeded.

Heck, even a small-town Indiana farm boy gains some smarts—after being tossed off the hay wagon or thrown off the proverbial turnip truck twice.

Again, when this door closed in my face—other doors quickly opened. An Indianapolis attorney, with whom I had been doing some international business, contacted me and said that he had an old friend who was the 2nd-generation owner of a printing company that was failing, and if help didn't arrive soon, the company would have to close its doors.

Well, I knew nothing about the printing business, but then again, I never had prior experience with *any* of the industries for the failing companies that I had previously turned around and rebuilt.

So, I signed an ironclad contract that, at my option, I could purchase the company, if I saved it from bankruptcy and got it turned around. The price was to be established by a certified audit, based on the day I stepped in the door as the company's new president.

Unfortunately, this company was also a "commodity" type printer that had no special capabilities and merely printed local restaurant menus, business cards, product brochures, and simple products that any other printer could produce.

By now, I had decades of experience behind me, and had tackled nearly every problem that a failing company might have. And, I had experienced all of the treachery that a 2nd-generation owner could throw at me.

I had worked in every department of those failing companies and learned firsthand why those companies were failing. I also learned the many ways that bad or dishonest management can rob, cheat, and steal from a company. It's called "Learning from the Good Ole Boys."

And then, things got worse—much worse! How bad were things on the first day I walked into the printing company?

Within the first four hours, I learned that the company had no money to make its payroll at the end of the week. Then, I learned that both of the company's banks had demanded that all outstanding loans be immediately repaid. This was on top of the fact that the company had $2.5 million of debt that was owed to a leasing company, for equipment that had been purchased from an Italian supplier who was no longer doing business in the United States. Wow, we owed $2.5 million for discontinued equipment that was no longer supported by the manufacturer!

On top of that bad news, the company's printing presses were sitting idle because the company's vendors wouldn't supply the paper and supplies that were needed to keep the company's presses running. Why? Because the company had not been paying its bills! The company's owner hadn't revealed any of these problems to me when he gave me a plant tour several weeks earlier—*when all of the printing presses were busy.*

How could this be, when the company's owner and his wife were driving around in gold-plated Cadillac and Lexus automobiles? They were living the life of the rich and famous—while their company was failing and ready to close its doors!

So my friends, I went from "Swimming with the Sharks," and trusting 2nd-generation owners—to this! It was like jumping out of a frying pan and into a fire. Wasn't this wonderful, and just what I was looking for? *Yeah, Right!* ☺

Some readers might think that I should I have turned around and walked back out the front door that I had just entered a few hours earlier. After all, why would any sane person want to become the president of a 2nd-generation family-owned businesses that was in this state of decline and ready to close its doors? It seemed that I was walking into another snake pit, after I had already been bitten, not once, but twice by 2nd-generation business owners!

Several professionals encouraged me to put the company through bankruptcy and stick it to the banks, suppliers, and other creditors. But, I had never taken advantage of others in the past, nor had I ever walked away from tough problems. And, I had always fully paid the financial debts that I owed to other people and to other companies. With my ethics and values, I was determined not to take advantage of the company's banks, suppliers, or creditors, and I was not going to quit on myself.

With the information I had gathered, I instinctively knew that if I saved the company from bankruptcy, the certified audit would conclude that the company had a zero book value—which, in fact, was proven to be the case.

As a result of learning the foregoing information during my first day with the company, I immediately contacted the company's two banks and requested meetings. At the first bank, the loan officer told me that all members of the company's management team were liars, and that he no longer believed anyone who represented the company. All he wanted was for our company to fully repay its loans. He had zero interest in helping us further. I informed him that the company had no ability to repay any of the debt that was currently owed to his bank—and couldn't even fund its current payroll.

The second banker was Daryl Moore, with Merchants National Bank. Daryl listened to me and checked into my background. He quickly confirmed my track record of success and chose to trust me.

The next day, Daryl called back and made a deal with me. He would lend the company more money, if I would put $30,000 into the company to meet that week's payroll, and if the current owner would pledge his personal liquid assets in support of a new loan. With this agreement in place, we got the business operating again, to support the meager level of sales that were trickling in.

Bankers like Daryl Moore are rare. His local bank was acquired several years later by Old National Bank, the largest bank holding company in Indiana. Daryl is now a senior vice president of that bank. Old National Bank obtained a great leader in Daryl Moore when they made that acquisition. Daryl was one of the true Heroes I met during my career. *Thank you, Daryl, for believing in me!*

The next thing I did was show the employees in the shop that I was on their team and was there to support them. In addition to talking to each employee, I personally started cleaning their filthy bathrooms.

I washed the boogers off the walls, scraped poop off the floors, replaced broken toilet seats, and cleaned the filthy restrooms with bleach. I then repainted the restrooms. How can management expect employees to support and respect them, if management doesn't show the same support and respect for each and every one of their employees? Some owners and managers never learn. They go through life thinking that "It's all about them"—while they drive around in their gold-plated Cadillac and Lexus automobiles, and act like rich and famous people!

My actions made all the difference in the world to our employees, who, until then, felt as though no one cared and that they were going to lose their jobs.

You see, this is another great value of being raised on a farm—I learned how to work (very hard), and no job was beneath me. In fact, my attitude was that if I didn't want to do the dirty jobs, then why should I expect anyone else to do them?

I knew how to clean up messes from our farm animals, which made the cleaning of human bathrooms a normal task for me. And, wasn't this exactly what I had been doing for most of my career—cleaning up crap that was created and left by the owners of other failing companies? As you can see, I still had all of the values and work ethic that I learned as a small-town farm boy.

Earlier in this book, I mentioned that "Birds of a Feather Flock Together." Well, I had just entered a company that was run by Good Ole Boys who were determined to get rid of me before I found out that they were the reason this company was failing. I received zero support from the existing management team—and I mean *Zero!*

That is what bad management does; its primary goal is to get rid of the new president as quickly as possible, so they can preserve their paychecks and return to the status quo. Remember, most companies fail because of bad management. And, this company was no exception! *These folks clearly exemplified the "Crab Mentality" that was discussed earlier in this book.*

It turned out that the company was a den of thieves. We had salespeople who were receiving a guaranteed paycheck from us every week, while taking many of their sales to other printing companies, where they were paid a commission for each sale they made. These folks were getting paid by two companies, for the same work. The result was that we were being scammed by many of our own salespeople. *They were stealing from us!*

I knew where and how to look for fraud. I discovered that a senior executive had sold company equipment, including printing presses, and used the proceeds to make payments on his mother's home mortgage and to pay for his gambling debts in Las Vegas—where he was considered to be a valued customer, who received free rooms, free dinners, and free alcoholic drinks. In addition to gambling trips to Las Vegas, this executive used company money to pay for a vacation to Disney World in Florida, with seven members of his family.

This same executive and another manager were selling our scrap materials for cash and pocketing the money. Another senior manager was getting kickbacks from suppliers, while the company was paying outrageous prices for their printing paper. One such kickback was in the form of a new Harley Davidson motorcycle that had been delivered as a Christmas present, just a few months earlier!

Well, it quickly became clear that this 2nd-generation business owner had lied to me about the financial condition of the business—or he was totally clueless, or both! Although he provided me with a "Certified Audit" for the prior two years, I found out that the company's Controller had previously worked for the CPA firm that performed the audit—and that the books were "cooked," with uncollectable receivables, some of which were more than five years old, from companies that had gone out of business. In addition, this failing company had assets listed on its financial books that no longer existed, because they had been sold by members of the management team, to pay off their personal debts.

With my experience at previous companies, I was able to stop this financial bleeding within four months. I knew what questions to ask, and I knew where theft usually takes place in a company. Most people think it takes place in the Accounting Department. Not so! The big dollars of theft usually take place with employees who do the sales, purchasing, or manage the company's operations. These are the folks who have access to suppliers and others who will offer them "gifts" in return for benefits that they receive.

Within six months, nearly all of these scoundrels left the company, on their own volition. I did not have to fire them, because once they knew that I was on to their schemes, they quickly left the company before legal charges could be filed—which I could not afford to do anyway, because the company was insolvent.

One ironic side-note is that most of these thieves got hired by our competitors—all of which went out of business while we rebuilt our failing company into a national leader during the next fifteen years.

Due to the many changes made during my first six months as president, we became profitable—and never had a losing year thereafter.

As previously stated: *"The American Dream Is Real, if you are willing to pay the price."* And, what a price I paid! But now, I was about to pay an even higher price.

My type of career takes a heavy toll on everyone. It was at this time that a major change took place in my life. As a result, I gave up every dime I had to start my personal life over. And, I mean every dime. I gave up my home, my car, my life savings—everything. I slept on my office floor, because at that time the company needed every dime I could save, just to survive. So, I guess you could say that not only were there some potholes in the road I traveled through this life—but there were also some huge sinkholes that shook my soul to its core.

Soon thereafter, our good Lord had the compassion to send an angel to my rescue. This angel had a print-management degree from Indiana State University and had been managing a small printing company where the absentee owners used the company as their money machine, while abusing her with low pay and unreasonable working hours.

Now, this young lady (I'll call her "Angel") could have had nearly any job she wanted in the printing industry, because she not only knew how to manage the operations—but after college, she gained invaluable sales experience as a print broker in Chicago. Yet, she chose to join our company, even though she knew that we were in a turnaround situation. The only thing I could promise was that, if we succeeded in rebuilding the company, she would receive an ownership interest. *She trusted me, and the rest is history—and the best part of my life.*

While I ran the production operations, Angel immediately began working to strengthen our customer-service policies, practices, and procedures. She then got into sales and quickly became our VP of Sales. Some of the remaining non-performing members of our sales staff chose to leave, rather than to rise to a higher level of performance that would justify their paychecks.

As with each of my previous turnaround companies, I was determined to rebuild this company by incorporating new technology into the business.

With this strategy in mind, Angel and I landed our first major publishing client, by promising to bring all of the intricate finishing operations that were needed for their fancy book covers into our manufacturing facilities. Until then, there was an unwritten rule in our local printing industry, and that was: "Printers print, and specialty finishers do the finishing"—such as UV coatings, foil stamping, embossing, film laminating, etc.

Our commitment to bring these intricate and decorative finishing operations in-house enraged the Indiana printing and finishing community. They blackballed us and refused to do any finishing work for us. To counter this disruption, until we brought all of these processes into our shop and gained sufficient expertise to complete our customers' orders, we had to load our truck and drive to Chicago to obtain the finishing work that our clients needed.

Week after week, and month after month, I was the person who drove our truck to Chicago. While the work was being done at night, I slept in the front seat, until I could return with our customer's finished book covers later that night or early the next morning. When the finishing jobs couldn't be done overnight, I had to make two trips to Chicago—one to deliver the printing to the specialty finisher and a second to pick up the jobs when they were finished. Either way, these trips were always made at night—because with our company on financial life-support, we couldn't afford to pay an employee to do this extra, but essential, work. Then, after returning the next morning, I had to oversee and manage the day-to-day operations at our printing facilities.

So, here was another hard lesson from my life: *"Not everything that happens to us in life is fair! But, no one can make us fail, if we have the determination and commitment to succeed." So, get over it, accept reality, and get on with pursuing your "American Dream!" And, that is exactly what we did.*

And, we did succeed! Over time, we acquired entry-level equipment and mastered each of the specialty-finishing processes that our publishing customers needed. By doing so, we were able to guarantee better quality and quicker deliveries—while providing our customers with huge savings, by cutting their purchasing costs for book covers by as much as 40%. How could we do this? Simple! We did not have to pay the exorbitantly high rates charged by the specialty finishers, who were part of the local "Good-Ole-Boy Network" that we despised in the printing and finishing industry! Therefore, we passed those savings on to our newly acquired publisher. They were overjoyed and gave us more and more of their work!

We started by supplying the specialty covers for Microsoft computer books for Pearson. We were then awarded all of the very fancy covers for their computer-game books and for the "Idiot's Guide" book series. In turn, this led to an introduction at their corporate headquarters in New Jersey, where we became a key supplier of high-quality book covers and specialty training and testing materials for their education markets. Jeff Valler, of Pearson Publishing, you were a Hero to us. Angel and I will never forget how important you were to our success.

Angel and I began attending the annual National Educators and Publishers Convention—only to learn that this convention was really a gathering of publishers who were wined and dined by the large book printers, with endless parties, to which Angel and I were never invited. We were just small puppies, trying to run with the Big Dogs, and no one in this close-knit group wanted to spend time meeting with us—nor would they toss us a bone! ☺

After three of these meetings and having achieved no success toward expanding our services onto a nationwide platform, Angel and I left for our return trip home, in a hotel van that made one more stop before we reached the airport. This last stop was another major turning point for our company!

A gentleman got into the van. We turned around and spoke to him, and learned that he had also attended the National Educators and Publishers Convention. As we expanded our conversation, we learned that he was Soma Coulibaly, the Vice President of Procurement for Houghton Mifflin, a large education publisher based in Boston. It was on that ride to the airport that Mr. Coulibaly invited himself to a visit at our plant in Terre Haute, Indiana.

By this time in our rebuilding process, we had upgraded a significant portion of our manufacturing equipment and had become a technology beta site for several international software and equipment manufacturers.

After visiting our manufacturing operations and understanding that we were a genuine, high-quality printer and finisher, Soma gave us an opportunity to work with his company. During our years with him, we saved Houghton Mifflin a significant amount of money and never had a late delivery or quality problem.

Soma was a fair, but very demanding buyer. He was a Hero to us, in even bigger ways, as you will soon learn.

Soma wanted to challenge the boundaries of technology by publishing textbooks with "printing over 3-D Registered Holograms." This is something that no company in the world had ever achieved when using high-speed, printing presses.

There were two reasons for wanting this technology for the education textbooks that Houghton Mifflin published. First, it would give them a unique-looking book cover that no other publisher in the world had ever achieved. Second, it would make it impossible for "pirates" to copy their textbooks, have them printed overseas, and then sell them at a lower price on the black market.

The reason this technology had never been used before was that there was no way to apply a 3-D Registered Hologram on a sheet of paper at high speed, in a process that was so precise that, each time the paper was run through a printing press, it would produce an accurate register of the ink to the hologram. We are talking about precision that is within one-ten thousandth of an inch. Very precise!

Well, our company and a much larger competitor from New York and Pennsylvania were given an equal opportunity to perfect this technology. Unfortunately, the companies that made the 3-D Holograms and stamping dies for Houghton Mifflin's project refused to work with us and chose to work exclusively with our larger competitor. So, we were left to develop this technology with no assistance from the major domestic suppliers who were involved with this project. We had to fend for ourselves. We knew that, if our larger competitor succeeded while we failed, it would be very detrimental to the future of our business.

After months of work on this project with other suppliers of Registered Holograms, we believed that we could achieve success. Then, we received Bad News—Houghton Mifflin was going to drop the project, because our larger competitor and the Houghton

Mifflin suppliers of the hologram foil and stamping dies had concluded that this new process was technically impossible to achieve.

Therefore, if this huge competitor (who was the industry leader) and the leading foil and stamping-die suppliers couldn't achieve success, then the process must be impossible to achieve—right?

We begged Soma Coulibaly to give us one chance to produce printed covers with the 3-D Registered Hologram technology. "Please, just give us one chance!"

On a Monday, Soma gave us that chance. Our East Coast competitor was instructed to send the stamping dies and hologram foil to us by Wednesday. In turn, we were to have finished covers at Houghton Mifflin's headquarters in Boston by the following Monday.

Well, Wednesday came and went. The competitor did not send the materials that we needed to proceed with this "impossible" job. We informed Soma Coulibaly—who then demanded that our competitor deliver the Registered Holograms and stamping dies to our shop by Friday, with a requirement that we still deliver finished covers to Houghton Mifflin on Monday.

Friday came and went; still no materials from our competitor. We received the hologram foil and stamping dies on Saturday, two days before we had to deliver finished book covers to the publisher, in Boston. This would have been a nearly impossible task, even if we had been supplying a normal book cover. But these covers were "impossible" to produce, according the world's leading experts.

Angel and I had a group of incredibly dedicated employees. We were determined not to fail. After using our secret process to stamp the holograms (developed internally), we printed and finished the covers on Saturday and Sunday—working 24 hours, around the clock. We rushed the covers to the airport and flew them to Boston. The folks at Houghton Mifflin were shocked!

Our huge East Coast competitor and the domestic companies that had been working with them were not only shocked—but they were embarrassed, very embarrassed! They told Houghton Mifflin's management that we were trying to pull some kind of scam on them—and that the process was impossible.

Soma Coulibaly then sent one of his production staff members to our plant to observe our processes. This person was shocked that we were being successful with our newly developed processes. Why was he shocked? Well, our large competitor had a sales office next door to Houghton Mifflin in Boston. These salespeople became very close friends with the Houghton Mifflin staff. Together, they did not want us to succeed. Therefore, upon returning to Houghton Mifflin in Boston, this guy reported that our processes were horrible!

However, by this time, Soma trusted Angel and me more than he trusted his own employees—so he gave us an exclusive purchase order to produce these very unique book covers. If we failed to produce the high-quality finished covers for this order, Houghton Mifflin would have incurred a very significant financial loss—and we would have lost this very important customer, forever!

We did get the job done—and produced outstanding book covers for this project. Upon release, the social studies textbooks with our printed 3-D Registered Hologram covers were a huge national marketing success for Houghton Mifflin. With this order, our company became the first and only company in the world to successfully apply and print on 3-D Registered Holograms, while using high-speed printing equipment.

Our larger East Coast competitor was livid! Until now, they had controlled the book-cover market with the education publishers. Now, those days of controlling the marketplace were over. Later, they tried to buy our company, to obtain our manufacturing technology, but we did not sell to them. They were so desperate that they even asked us to supply them with finished book covers, using our technology, for sale to some of their other publishing clients. We did them a huge favor and printed their covers. Again, those were our values and ethics.

Thank you, Soma Coulibaly. You believed in us and gave us an opportunity to succeed big time in the education-publishing industry. You were a Hero to us!

The foregoing is further proof that "Life Is Not About Me." Our success in life happened because we met the needs of other people and other companies, and we did it better than any of our competitors.

With the advances we were bringing to the education and computer-publishing industry and our company's positive reputation in the marketplace, our volume was growing rapidly. Our production plants were running around the clock, seven days a week, to complete and ship incoming orders. Therefore, we had to upgrade all of our prepress and press equipment, which was very expensive. The price for each of our new printing presses was between $1 million and $2 million. As we upgraded our operations, we partnered with leading firms throughout the world and became a beta site for new technologies in our industry. It was rather easy to obtain these new technology partnerships, because, by this time, we had achieved a national reputation as a high-tech print communications company.

Along the way, other major education publishers became our clients and found that our firm could provide them with the best quality, on-time deliveries, and lower prices.

Then, the VP of Global Sourcing for the National Geographic Society (NGS) contacted us via email and wanted to visit our plant. We thought that this inquiry was a cruel joke and that a prankster was just playing around with us. But, this inquiry turned out to be real. We couldn't believe that the head of global procurement for NGS, the top-quality publisher in the world, wanted to visit our plant! This was beyond any dream we could have envisioned!

The NGS Vice President arrived within two weeks, and after spending the day at our facilities, he said, "You guys do great work, but you are too small to handle all of our high-quality work." We responded by saying, "Give us a chance—and you will be glad that you did."

The rest is history. Within nine months, we became a key supplier to NGS. We never missed a delivery date and never had a quality problem.

During this time period, Angel was featured as one of the *Top Ten Women Business Entrepreneurs in America by* **Printing Impressions,** *the national magazine for the printing industry.* *What an honor!*

With all of this activity, we never had a moment to kick back and relax. Angel and I worked seven days a week for 15 years, and never had a week of vacation.

As discussed in Chapter 17, as entrepreneurs, we are never truly our own boss. We have responsibilities to our employees, our customers, our suppliers, our banks, our community—and for many others.

Therefore, Angel and I put the care and needs of others first—before we thought of ourselves. It was a lot like being raised on our farm in Hoagland, Indiana, where my brothers and I had the responsibility of taking care of the daily needs of our farm animals. Fulfilling these daily chores is something every farmer must do, if he wishes to be successful.

This reminds me of the old adage about farm boys—which is very true: *"You can take the boy from the farm, but you can't take* *the farm from the boy."* The values and work ethic we developed on the farm are essential for every entrepreneur and career-focused adult, if they expect to excel in their business or profession.

As stated earlier in this book:

"The American Dream Is Real, if you are willing to pay the price."

We paid a very high price for our success in achieving the "American Dream."

The American Dream Is Real

If You Are Willing To Pay The Price

CHAPTER 43

Time To Move On

Living the "American Dream" does not mean working for money until we leave this Earth. Living the "American Dream" has a lot to do with moving on—to new challenges and opportunities that enrich us and make our lives more fulfilling.

Unfortunately, many family business owners think that they will live forever and fail to plan for the future of their company. I saw this happen many times during my professional career and was determined that this would not be a repeat story for Angel and me. Remember, Angel and I had not had a single week of vacation for 15 years, while we saved and rebuilt our company into a national leader. We also entered the export market—which was unheard of by most of our competitors.

As I look back over my career, I never witnessed a business that was an "Overnight Success." In fact, *nearly all successful business owners spend at least 15 years, when building their "Overnight Success" story.*

So, in accordance with our own Personal Strategic Plan, it was time to transfer the ownership of our company—just as we reached the top of our performance and before we had to endure another expansion or transition through another generation of emerging technologies. Growing bigger (again) was something I did not want to experience, since I had already suffered a heart attack.

We sold our firm to a public company that was the 3rd-largest book manufacturer in the world. Together, our two companies had excellent synergism and no duplication of effort. Angel and I did not sell to a competitor, because we wanted our employees to have a good future with a book printer that needed our capabilities and expertise.

Had we sold to a major competitor, they probably would have kept our clients, taken our technologies, moved our production to one of their other facilities, and closed our sales and production operations. There was no way we were going to put our employees and their families in this kind of jeopardy.

On the day of closing, it seemed as though a major burden was lifted from our shoulders, but it had a tinge of sadness, because it was like watching our only child leave home for the next chapter in their life. Again, the feeling I got was similar to the Dick & Dee Dee song "Turn Around," in which they ponder how fast their children had grown up, and how quickly they left home to pursue their own lives.

From several mergers that I have personally experienced during my career, Angel and I decided to remain on-board during a transition period, and then retire. Experience has taught me that, when a large public company buys a smaller company, there is a consistent pattern of how the transition evolves.

During the first year of the merger, the new owner treats the management team from the acquired company as though they were God. Why? Simple—because the former owners (us) developed technologies and processes that the acquiring company never achieved. So, they need us badly, for a couple of years!

By the end of the second year of a merger, the buyer has completed installation of their reporting and administrative systems, brought their department managers and technical experts into our facilities to look over every aspect of our operations, and completed documenting everything they need to understand.

Then, by the end of the third year, the sellers are no longer God, because the new owners are now God! And sure enough, history repeated itself, and it was time for Angel and me to move on with the rest of our lives. But, this time we exited under our own free will, and it was our desire to do so. ☺

It is interesting how the experiences we accumulate over our lives can help us during each of the following segments of our career. I was happy to have the lifelong learning experiences that taught me what to expect following the merger. Those experiences were "Spot-On" and repeated themselves when we sold our company.

Had we not experienced the hardships of turning around other companies, and had we not been stabbed in the back by many of the people we trusted during our careers, I am not sure that we would have succeeded with the turnaround of this printing company and rebuilt it into a high-tech print communications company, with the finest reputation for technology, quality, service, and integrity in the industry. *Here again is proof that success in our career is heavily dependent on our reputations and with putting other peoples' needs ahead of our own needs, wants, and desires.*

This was a company that should have failed, and would have failed if this small-town farm boy and Angel had not been willing to step in and save the jobs of the existing employees—and then create many new jobs as we revitalized and re-envisioned the company with new technology, processes, and equipment.

As the Great Guru told the college graduate, "We make good decisions by learning from the mistakes we make." And, as you have read, I learned the hard way!

My naiveté that came from a small-town farming background caused me to pay a very dear price for my achievements. I got used, was kicked, and got knocked down many times, but each time I picked myself up—and as Coach Vince Lombardi would have expected, got back in the game and continued pursuing my dreams.

Stated another way, I got tossed from the proverbial hay wagon or turnip truck several times before I finally learned. Looking back, I have to laugh at my naiveté. It taught me that learning can be a very painful experience, but it can also be rewarding and very satisfying over time!

And, had I not had my prior experiences, I never would have met Angel—who made all of my past hardships and disappointments seem insignificant. *Angel is my "American Dream," and, together, we are "Living the American Dream."*

Now that we are retired, we thank God that we have found alternative passions, beyond our professional careers.

First, I thoroughly enjoy mentoring high school and college students with their career planning and entrepreneur classes, and with counseling small businesses.

Equally important, Angel works (volunteers for free) seven days a week, to save the lives of abandoned and abused puppies and kitties. Our spay/neuter program has greatly reduced the number of unwanted pets in our community, and we no longer have dog-packs roaming the hills and valleys of Brown County, Indiana.

Today, the Brown County Humane Society and its spay/neuter program are considered to be among the best success stories in animal rescue and care in the United States. Brown County residents are very proud of their humane society and the many volunteers who work tirelessly to save the lives of these abused and/or abandoned pets—and then find adopting families who will give them a loving, forever home. What a wonderful experience and feeling! Every community, town, and city should have this level of dedication. Why don't they? It's due solely to a lack of leadership in those communities—and nothing else.

And, unlike the human world, we have never found an unkind puppy or kitty. We find that they all give us more love than we can possibly give back to them. Most of these little tykes give us unconditional love. *And, we love their kisses!* ☺

Looking at it from another perspective, *is it possible that puppies are proof that there is a God?* After all, the kindness and love we receive from puppies is nearly universal—much better than the way many human beings treat each other. Maybe puppies are God's example to us—to show us how we should treat each other, in a kinder and more caring manner. What do you think?

So really, we are not working. Instead, we are continuing to help others live better lives, including puppies and kitties.

And "yes," Angel can, and still does, outwork me! She works at her volunteer job seven days a week, and I fully support her efforts. ☺

We are truly living the "American Dream," and so can you!

The American Dream

Is Real

But It

Must Be Earned

PART IV

Now, It's Time for Your American Dream

CHAPTER 4 4

The Passing of
the Torch to
Your Generation

So, young folks—there you have it. Now, I hope you will put the life of this small-town farm boy and small-town girl into perspective with your life.

If we could experience and achieve all of the foregoing in life, despite the fact that Angel and I were not born into families of privilege or wealth, and the fact that I graduated in the lower half of my high school class of 39 students from the small town of Hoagland, Indiana, then you, too, can achieve success and experience a lifetime of opportunity that is available in our wonderful United States of America.

Yes, from earlier chapters in this book, it is clear that "Life Is Not Fair." I experienced a lot of betrayals from people I trusted during my career. And, we all realize that our society and economic system are not perfect—and never will be perfect. Why?

Because our planet is populated by human beings—none of whom are perfect! I'm not perfect! Are you perfect, or are any of your friends perfect? Do you know anyone who is perfect? I don't. It's just like being born—none of us "asked to be born," and none of us on this Earth are perfect.

During my travels, I never visited another country where you or I could have the level of freedom and opportunity that we have in the United States—to reach for and achieve success that is beyond our wildest dreams. I thank my Creator every day! So, let's all make the best of our life while we are on this Earth. The opportunity is here—but *you must want it, plan for it, and you must earn it!*

Each time I reminisce about my worldwide travels, a song passes through my mind. The song is *"America the Beautiful,"* which states, *"America, America, God shed His grace on thee..."* Wow, what an accurate and emotionally moving statement about our wonderful country! *We are very blessed to live here.*

As I reflect back on my journey through this life, I am reminded of my wonderful high school basketball coach, Mark Schoeff, who said "Evan, after graduation, get as far away from Hoagland as you can, because there is a great big world out there for you to experience." Boy, was he right!

And, as Angel and I experienced during our careers, we hope you encounter many heroes along the way who are instrumental in helping to advance your career—as you find ways to help make their lives better. Those encounters were wonderful and more than made up for some of the hurts we experienced along the way. *Our Career Mentors and Heroes were Invaluable to us!*

Remember, life is not just about you or me and getting what we want. Yet, we can achieve nearly anything we want in life—if we find ways to help other people improve their lives.

And, it is important to realize that success can be achieved without sacrificing good morals, values, and ethics. Please make this your choice and commitment.

From my life's struggles, I now hope you understand why four of my American heroes are Harold McMaster, Dr. Ben Carson, Dr. Phil, and my wife, Angel. They all started with nothing, had no advantages handed to them—but all avoided playing the Victim role or using Excuses, while they pursued success with their "American Dream." Equally important, each of them had high values and lived a moral and ethical life.

Now, it is time for my generation to pass the torch—and help today's youth pursue their "American Dream."

As documented throughout this book, *"The American Dream is Not Free."* Like our formal education, it must be earned! Pursuing the American Dream is very much like pursuing a PhD. It requires:

P Personal Strategic Planning
H Hunger to succeed in life
D Determination to never quit on yourself!

Regardless of your circumstance in life, regardless of what others tell you about your lack of potential, and regardless of your lack of self-confidence—remember, you will have control over 80%–90% of what happens to you in your life.

The next 5–10 years will establish the foundation of education, knowledge, and skills you will offer to the world. You can make yourself valuable—but you will need a Personal Strategic Plan to guide you toward achieving the knowledge and training the world needs, because *each of us has to Earn Our American Dream.*

Currently, you might not have the best grades, and you might not be highly self-motivated. But, you can change that. *Your choices from this point forward will control your future. Remember, you are the CEO of your own personal company.* I took charge of my life after graduating high school—and changed my life by not listening to those who said that I would never be anything other than a small-town farm boy. I then pursued a two-year Associate Degree and grew from that knowledge. The rest of my life was unbelievable! As you know, I even met an "Angel" along the way! ☺

And, speaking of Angel, I hope everyone noticed the many successful women who were recognized in this book and in the testimonials. Some are in senior management positions, while others are internationally recognized scientists, teachers, registered nurses, or entrepreneurs. None of these highly successful people saw limits to their education or career possibilities and opportunities.

The future will require many more young women to pursue higher education and professional careers. Having helped many young women succeed during my career, it is my hope that the contents of this book will benefit many more young women and underachieving young boys, like me—who thought they had no future! ☺

Here is one last but very important observation for all young readers—it is the old adage that states, *"Whenever one door closes—another door opens."*

My life and my career are proof that this adage is true—but only because I obtained the education, training, and skills that I needed to provide a valuable service to other people and to other companies.

As a result, every time an unscrupulous business owner or private-equity company took advantage of my successful efforts to rebuild their company, and every time I had a company pulled out from under me—I never once had to apply for unemployment benefits or search long to find the next door that opened up!

My services and leadership were in high demand—because very few people had my education, training, or record of success. Understanding this factor can have a major impact on planning a successful future for today's youth.

In today's turbulent society, it is easy to get caught-up with the negativism that is being spewed about. Some people believe that America's greatness is over, and that my generation was lucky enough to live through the best days of America's history. *Don't believe this negativism about our beloved country and your future.*

I believe that America's best days are yet to come, and with the passing of the torch, my generation will support, help and guide today's youth toward achieving an even better future. But it will be up to each new generation to have the hunger, commitment, determination, and never-quit work ethic to make our free society an even better place to live. *Remember, the American Dream is Not Free, we must Earn It—and we must protect our freedoms from the false promises of Socialism, if we hope to achieve our American Dream.*

If today's youth are successful, not only will their lives be better—but they will then be able to pass on to future generations the very positive legacy of and even stronger and more prosperous country. *May this be the legacy that you leave for your children, grandchildren and the generations that follow you in this wonderful country we call the United States of America.*

So, what is your plan for the future? Have you started your Personal Strategic Plan? If not, please start. As another old adage states: *"If you fail to plan, then you are planning to fail."* Remember, you are in charge of your life, so please begin planning for a positive and productive future.

It is my hope that you will become a hero for the next generation that follows—just as my high school coach Mark Schoeff, Harold

McMaster, Dr. Ben Carson, Dr. Phil McGraw, and my wife, Angel became heroes in my life.

The American Dream Is Real. But, you must **earn it by getting your** "**PHD.**"

May God bless you on your path toward achieving the "American Dream."

The

American Dream Is Real

If

You Are Willing To Pay The Price

Loving Rescue Pups

About the Author
(Evan A. Werling)

The author of this book is living proof that, no matter how difficult life might be, everyone has an opportunity to achieve *"The American Dream."*

During his career, he experienced the fact that young women have a more difficult time, as they strive to achieve the "American Dream." He hired and promoted more women than men and taught the ethics and values it takes to succeed in a competitive world.

This small-town farm boy from Hoagland, Indiana had nothing going for him at the time he graduated in the lower half of his high school class of 39 students. Yet, through his own career planning, determination, and hard work, step-by-step, he picked himself up, changed his life, and achieved the "American Dream."

After graduating high school and leaving the farm, he worked and earned his way through a vocational school, and then graduated with Honors, at the top of the Business College at Ball State University. He took additional courses at other universities, including business law through Indiana University's MBA program.

He earned every penny to pay for his education and received no scholarships, government loans, or other financial support.

From his humble beginnings to a CPA and International Entrepreneur, Mr. Werling became a business-turnaround expert, and rebuilt failing companies into domestic and international leaders—without laying off a single employee.

While doing so, he testified before more than a dozen US Senate and House Committees, was nominated to be the United States Exporter of the Year by the US Chamber of Commerce, became the Ohio Exporter of the Year, and was awarded two Presidential "E" Awards for excellence in exporting. He has been an advisor to many state governors and was appointed to numerous national committees and boards. During his career, he was invited to breakfast with President Ronald Reagan and then to lunch by President George Herbert Walker Bush—both of whom he found to be wonderful gentlemen.

Today, Mr. Werling is a mentor to small businesses. He is also a mentor and speaker at various high schools and colleges. In this capacity, he reveals his secrets for success—among them is the fact that *"Life is Not About You or Me."* Instead, we gain respect and are rewarded for how we improve the lives of other people and other organizations. Once we learn this truth, the path for success becomes much clearer. As this small-town farm boy likes to say:

The American Dream Is Real

If

You Are Willing To Pay The Price